# RENAISSAN

## INTRODUCTION

A Victorian representation of the return of the survivors of Flodden to Edinburgh. The clothing and armour may be inaccurate, but the sense of shock and fear is palpable.

The first half of the 16th century witnessed two shattering defeats of the Scots by the English: at Flodden in 1513, and at Pinkie in 1547. But by March 1550 the artillery along the border had fallen silent, and the smoke cleared from the escarpments at Lauder. The English garrison – starving, reduced to melting down pewter cups to make harquebus-shot, and with no hope of relief – struck their colours and departed. The English had been expelled from every notable garrison north of the border. The Debateable Lands would continue to be the scene of border violence for the next 50 years, but the English and Scottish armies would never again face each other in the field. (In fact, the next major English army to cross the border would do so to help the Scottish Protestant lords force the French out of the country.) The Scottish war machine, despite being soundly beaten in every major encounter, had prevailed at the last.

This book is principally concerned with the organization, arms, equipment and tactics of Scottish armies during those years of rapid change; but to put these into context we must first look at some of the campaigns and battles that best illustrate the Scottish strategy and tactics of the period, and that define the military environment in which the armies had to wage war.

## CAMPAIGNS & BATTLES

### The Road to Flodden

The Treaty of Perpetual Peace was endorsed by the marriage of King James IV of Scotland to Margaret, the daughter of King Henry VII of England, in 1502. James was a worthy suitor: since his succession in 1488 he had proved to be a well-liked and

James IV had proven to be a true king of the Renaissance, embracing all that was modern; he loved jousting, but also music and the sciences – he had even tried his hand at surgery. He was an artillery enthusiast, and was fascinated by all things nautical; by 1513 he had built up the most powerful Scottish army and navy yet seen. (© National Galleries of Scotland. Licensor www.scran.ac.uk.)

reliable king who had embraced the new age with great enthusiasm, and had implemented a series of innovative political strategies. He had reined in the Lords of the Western Isles, and exercised a degree of control over the turbulent Borders; he even planned a crusade to wrest control of the Mediterranean from the Ottoman Turks. Scotland was prosperous and thriving; but since James always had to be wary of his unruly nobility, he had been happy to conclude a seven-year peace agreement with England in 1497. This also suited the cautious and parsimonious Henry Tudor; but events on the continent of Europe were soon to drag Scotland and England into confrontation once more.

In 1494 King Charles VIII of France had invaded Italy to claim the papal state of Naples for himself, thus sparking off a series of wars that would last for decades, involving a new generation of players after the original antagonists had died. In 1498 Charles of France went to his grave, and was succeeded by his son Louis XII. In 1510 the pugnacious Pope Julius II formed a new Holy League against France, and the following year he offered inducements to bring the hot-headed young Henry VIII of England – himself just two years on the throne – into the League. James of Scotland worked hard to bring Louis and Pope Julius to the negotiating table, but to no avail, and the papacy remained intransigent even after Julius died in March 1513, to be succeeded by Leo X. Soon Henry and the Holy Roman Emperor, Maximilian, were intriguing with the Vatican against France, and King Louis was offering James IV persuasive reasons to resume Scotland's traditional policy of hostility towards England. With French funds on offer, James started building up a massive armoury and artillery train out of his new workshops in Edinburgh; he sanctioned privateering by his sea captains on the English merchant fleet, and in November 1512 he felt obliged to renew the 'Auld Alliance' with the French.

There followed a year of positioning as James played for time to improve military resources that he recognized were antiquated. He called upon Louis for the promised gold, but none was forthcoming: the French coffers were being drained to counter the threat of the Emperor Maximilian's armies, but Louis did send practical help in the form of 40 captains under the Sieur d'Aussi to train the Scots in the modern ways of war, and these veterans landed in Dumbarton along with shipments of pikes, harquebuses (handguns) and artillery.

In June 1513, Henry of England set sail for France in support of Maximilian, leaving the defence of the North to the old but vigorous Thomas Howard, Earl of Surrey, a veteran of the battles of Barnet and Bosworth. James of Scotland responded immediately by despatching his navy to France (via Carrickfergus Castle, which was bombarded in an abortive attempt to support the rising of Irish rebels). The muster was called, and the Scots levy flooded towards Edinburgh on a tide of national fervour; over 30,000 men gathered at Boroughmuir before moving south.

Elite • 167

# Scottish Renaissance Armies 1513–1550

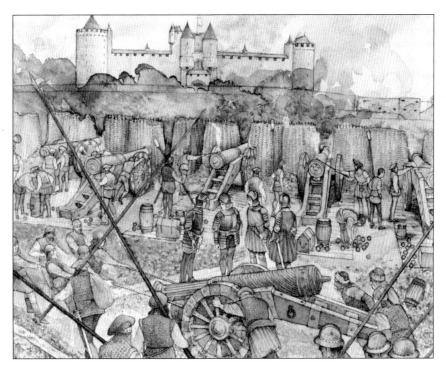

Jonathan Cooper • Illustrated by Graham Turner

Consultant editor Martin Windrow

First published in Great Britain in 2008 by Osprey Publishing,
Midland House, West Way, Botley, Oxford OX2 0PH, UK
443 Park Avenue South, New York, NY 10016, USA

Email: **info@ospreypublishing.com**

ISBN: 978 1 84603 325 4

Editor: Martin Windrow
Page layout by Ken Vail Graphic Design, Cambridge, UK
Typeset in Helvetica Neue and ITC New Baskerville
Index by Mike Parkin
Originated by PPS Grasmere, Leeds, UK
Printed in China through World Print Ltd.

08 09 10 11 12    10 9 8 7 6 5 4 3 2 1

A CIP catalogue record for this book
is available from the British Library

FOR A CATALOGUE OF ALL BOOKS PUBLISHED BY OSPREY MILITARY AND
AVIATION PLEASE CONTACT:

NORTH AMERICA:
Osprey Direct
c/o Random House Distribution Center, 400 Hahn Road, Westminster,
MD 21157
E-mail: info@ospreydirectusa.com

ALL OTHER REGIONS:
Osprey Direct UK,
PO Box 140, Wellingborough, Northants NN8 2FA, UK
E-mail: info@ospreydirect.co.uk

Buy online at **www.ospreypublishing.com**

Osprey Publishing is supporting the Woodland Trust, the UK's leading
woodland conservation charity, by funding the dedication of trees.

## Acknowledgements

Special thanks must go to Dr David Caldwell at the National
Museum of Scotland, and Dr Tony Pollard and Dr Iain Banks
at the Centre for Battlefield Archaeology at Glasgow
University, for their inspiration, support and advice. Many
thanks must also go to Graham Turner for bringing the
sketches to life.

## Dedication

To my parents, my children and, most of all, my wife Alison,
for supporting me in my passion.

## Artist's Note

Readers may care to note that the original paintings from
which the colour plates in this book were prepared are
available for private sale. All reproduction copyright
whatsoever is retained by the Publishers. All enquiries
should be addressed to:

*Graham Turner*
*PO Box 568,*
*Aylesbury,*
*Buckinghamshire*
*HP17 8ZX,*
*UK*

The Publishers regret that they can enter into no
correspondence upon this matter.

## Flodden Field, 1513

James's declaration of war was delivered to Henry at Therouanne in northern France on 11 August 1513. Two days later, under the cover of a violent storm, 8,000 Scots commanded by Alexander Home, Warden of the Marches, crossed the border on the River Tweed to lay waste to local villages. As they headed north again, burdened with booty, they were ambushed by Sir William Bulmer and some 1,000 horse-archers and Border horsemen. Caught between two wings of bowmen, some 500 Scots were killed and 300 more taken prisoner; the survivors of what became known as the 'Ill Raid' slunk back across the border empty-handed.

By 18 August the main Scottish army was on the move; it marched towards the English border stronghold of Norham Castle where, after six days, the garrison was battered into submission. Etal, Chillingham and Ford went the same way; James now had time to choose his ground and await the English. Flodden Edge, about 5 miles inside England, was a formidable obstacle, blocking the English advance and threatening any flank march along the coast; James's eastwards-facing position, surmounted by temporary fortifications and bristling with his artillery, was apparently impregnable. The English refused to oblige with a frontal assault, and on 9 September Surrey hooked around the eastern flank of the Scottish position, getting between the Scots and the border. James, outmanoeuvred, was forced to pull back down the ridge and take up another strong position on the rain-lashed slopes of Branxton Hill, overlooking the deploying English army to his north-west.

The battle opened on the afternoon of 9 September with an artillery duel in which the English, having lighter guns and more practised crews, outshot their Scottish counterparts. As the English artillery turned their

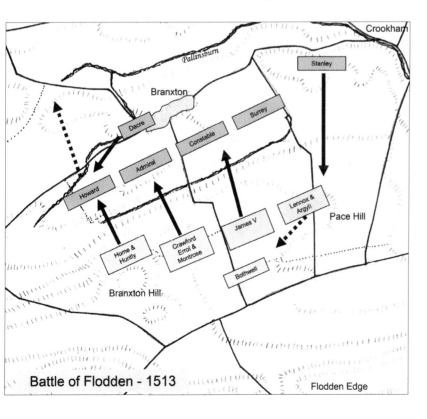

Battle of Flodden - 1513

The Scottish army descended from Branxton Hill in echelon. Their left division crashed into the smaller English ward and put it to rout, but a counter-attack by the English horse led by Lord Dacre held up the Scottish advance. The remaining Scottish wards floundered in the ditch and mire in front of the English position; then Stanley's ward broke Lennox's highlanders, before rolling up the Scottish right. (Author's collection)

KING·JAMES·5ᵗ
NAT·1512·OB·1542

James V spent most of his teens in the custodianship of his stepfather, Archibald Douglas, Earl of Angus. In 1526, at the age of 14, he witnessed the death of his favoured uncle the Earl of Lennox at Linlithgow as a result of Angus' orders; this was something he would never forget or forgive. (© National Galleries of Scotland)

fire on the Scottish infantry, James believed the time was right to set his pike blocks in motion. The left 'battle' or 'ward', under the command of Lord Home and the Earl of Huntly, advanced first, and had an uninterrupted run at their opponents on the English right. Descending in 'Almayn' manner, with their pikes lowered, the heavily armoured Scots pikemen withstood the desultory English archery and crashed into Edmund Howard's outnumbered Cheshire and Lancashire levies. Howard himself was almost overrun, but Lord Dacre, with some 1,500 English Border horse, cut their way through to his rescue.

Inspired by the success on their left, the remaining Scottish 'battles' now quickened their pace . King James dismounted and joined his lairds on the front rank, such was his confidence in the outcome. The ward commanded by the Earls of Crawford and Montrose should have been the next to hit home; but the steeper, slippery slope and the weight of their armour slowed their advance, and the pike block lost momentum as they struggled out of an unforeseen depression in front of the English lines. The English responded in perfect order and with consummate timing, the Lord Admiral's men crashing into the floundering Scottish throng. With their momentum lost the Scottish levies threw down their pikes and drew their swords, but these were easily outreached by the bills of their adversaries, and the English started the bloody, drawn-out process of felling the Scottish ranks.

James's own battle fared little better; the Scottish attack ground to a halt, despite his personal leadership of a desperate charge toward Surrey's standard. The king was chopped down, almost unnoticed in the mêlée, and his body was so hacked that it would be unrecognizable to his followers. The final 'ward', under Lennox and Argyll, consisted mainly of lightly armed Highland troops who, without direction, failed to charge home and were flanked by Stanley's retinue. Hemmed in by the slopes of Branxton Hill, bogged down in the mire in the depression, and leaderless, the Scottish army was butchered; only Home and Huntly were able to extricate their men and cover the retreat. Nine earls, 14 lords of parliament and 79 other gentry died with their king, along with an estimated 6,000 other Scottish fighting men. The survivors fled to the border, and did not stop until they reached Edinburgh.

### Linlithgow Bridge, 1526

James V was 17 months old when his father was cut down at Flodden, and the Scottish parliament called upon John Stuart, Duke of Albany, to act as regent during the king's minority. Albany held the office as best he could for the next ten years, despite the political in-fighting of the lairds and the intrigues of the French and English kings. However, an abortive winter raid on Wark in 1523 was the last straw for Albany: his force of 3,000 Frenchmen was repelled by an English garrison of 140 men. Faced with flagging support at home, and unable to convince his French paymasters to supply more arms and men, Albany retired to the continent for good.

Into the political void stepped James V's stepfather, Archibald Douglas, 6th Earl of Angus. In February 1525, after years of exile in England, Angus rode into Edinburgh at the head of his own retinue and those of John Stewart, 3rd Earl of Lennox, and Sir Walter Scott of Buccleuch. He persuaded parliament that the custodianship of the king should be by rota, with four lairds at a time looking after the child in succession – naturally, Angus himself would lead the first group. Parliament agreed, and Angus took the boy into his care; he quickly surrounded the king with his own allies, and refused to hand him on at the end of his stint.

Now confident in his grip on the throne, Angus declared his royal stepson's minority to be at an end; but he had not taken into consideration the teenager's temperament, and James V immediately declared his uncle, Lennox, as his favoured advisor. Lennox accepted the role with some trepidation, but organized an attempt to snatch the king when the royal party headed south to Melrose in July 1526. He arranged for Walter Scott of Buccleuch to ambush them at Darnock Tower; however, the Borderers preferred to face the Douglases in a stand-up fight. They were soundly beaten, Scott was wounded, and Lennox was forced to leave court hastily.

The Hamilton and Douglas troops surge down upon the Lennox retinue men and highlanders at the battle of Linlithgow Bridge. (Alan Gault)

Lennox's drive towards Edinburgh was held up at Linlithgow by the local forces raised by the Earl of Arran. Lennox was forced to cross upstream at Manuel Convent, before heading back towards the West Port. However, Arran's outnumbered men held off the rebels until victory was secured by the timely arrival of Angus and his Douglas reinforcements from Edinburgh. (Author's collection)

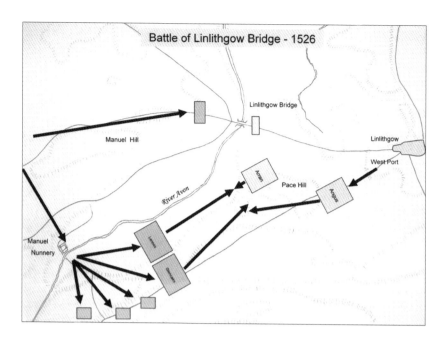

Lennox rode hard for Stirling and, with the queen-mother's backing, raised an army of some 10,000 men which included the Earls of Glencairn, Cassilis, Eglington and Crawford, many of the lairds of Fife, the 'West Lands' and his Highland factions. Lennox set off for Edinburgh on 3 September 1526. In his way stood James Hamilton, Earl of Arran, who had defected to the Douglas cause during the summer. Arran raised some 3,000 men from the local burghs, fortified the bridge across the Avon about 2 miles west of Linlithgow, and deployed his men on the strategically important Pace Hill overlooking the main routes into the town.

Lennox approached the bridge on 4 September; seeing the strength of its defence, he left his heavier artillery and a holding force in place, then marched upstream to the ford at Manuel Nunnery. There he forced the crossing and had his troops form up into two battles, led by himself and Glencairn; Lennox then ordered an advance on the Hamilton position. The Hamiltons held on to the high ground despite being outnumbered, and victory was assured when Angus arrived with 3,000 reinforcements from Edinburgh. The wounded Lennox surrendered his sword, but was then brutally murdered by James Hamilton of Finnart. Glencairn was also wounded, but was taken to safety by Sir Andrew Wood of Largo, who had been despatched by the king to save as many of the rebels as he could. There are no records of exact casualties for the action, but certainly the pursuit of the fugitives went on well into the night. Angus then marched on Stirling and Dunfermline in order to intercept the queen-mother and her co-conspirators, but they had already taken to the hills.

The young King James realized that he would have to make his own plans to get free of his Douglas guardians. Eventually, in 1528, he escaped from Edinburgh and made his way to Stirling, where he was met by his mother and the lords now declaring their loyalty to him; at the age of 16, his years of minority were truly over. Angus, after avoiding capture at the siege of his castle at Tantallon, fled south to exile at the English court of his brother-in-law, and James V's uncle, Henry VIII. In the years that followed James' policy moved increasingly towards a pro-French stance – particularly after he married first a French princess and then, after her early death, a French duchess.

## Loch Lochy, 1544

James V's later suppression of the Highlands was brutal and effective; a grand naval tour of 1540 enabled him to strike at many coastal strongholds, leaving a trail of fear and resentment amongst the Highland leaders, many of whom now languished in Lowland gaols. After this emphatic show of strength there was relative peace in the Highlands, but James would have little time to profit by it. In December 1542 – shortly after the defeat of a Scottish by an English army at Solway Moss on 24 November, and just a week after the birth of his daughter Mary – James V died at the age of 30.

Once again the country was plunged into long years of an uncertain minority, as Scottish affairs sank once more into their habitual state of internecine quarrels among the nobility. This time it was the vacillating James Hamilton, 2nd Earl of Arran, who took over the regency, despite the scheming of the widowed Queen Mary of Guise and

James V died in December 1542 at Falkland Palace – it is said, of despair, after the death of his sons in childhood, and the defeat of the Scottish army at Solway Moss. He left his six-day old daughter Mary as his heir. (© National Galleries of Scotland. Licensor www.scran.ac.uk.)

Clan warfare raged throughout the first half of the 16th century. Many skirmishes have been lost to history, and those that were recorded are often clouded in legend.

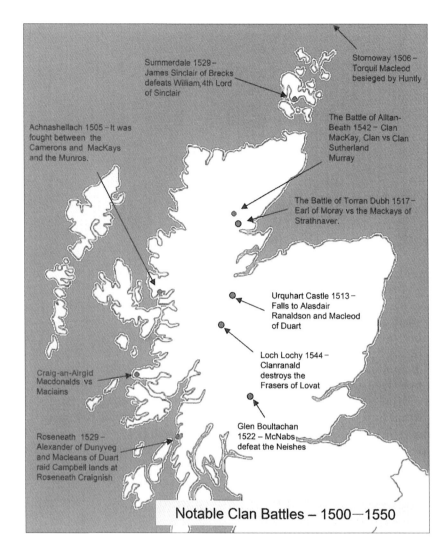

Summerdale 1529 – James Sinclair of Brecks defeats William, 4th Lord of Sinclair

Stornoway 1506 – Torquil Macleod besieged by Huntly

Achnashellach 1505 – It was fought between the Camerons and MacKays and the Munros.

The Battle of Alltan-Beath 1542 – Clan MacKay, Clan vs Clan Sutherland Murray

The Battle of Torran Dubh 1517 – Earl of Moray vs the Mackays of Strathnaver.

Urquhart Castle 1513 – Falls to Alasdair Ranaldson and Macleod of Duart

Loch Lochy 1544 – Clanranald destroys the Frasers of Lovat

Craig-an-Airgid Macdonalds vs Maciains

Glen Boultachan 1522 – McNabs defeat the Neishes

Roseneath 1529 – Alexander of Dunyveg and Macleans of Duart raid Campbell lands at Roseneath Craignish

### Notable Clan Battles – 1500–1550

Cardinal David Beaton. Family rivalries, and those between pro-French and pro-English parties, were now compounded by the religious divisions between Lutherans and Catholics. The Highland clans again rose up in arms, egged on by Henry VIII and his 'Assured Scots' (Scots in English pay), and many of the lairds taken at Solway Moss were released, returning north to champion a pro-English agenda. Amongst the familiar faces attending court was Archibald Douglas, 6th Earl of Angus, back from his second period of exile in England. It was this pro-English faction that persuaded Arran to sign the Treaty of Greenwich in 1543, retaining Mary in Scotland until she was aged ten but promising her in marriage to Henry's son, Edward. For his part, Cardinal Beaton engineered the return to court of Mathew Stewart, 4th Earl of Lennox, in order to undermine Arran's grip on the stewardship. Arran was also opposed by Archibald Campbell, 4th Earl of Argyll, and George Gordon, 4th Earl of Huntly, the main players in the North. In response, Arran set about undermining his enemies by releasing many of the Highland lairds imprisoned by James V, including John Moidertach of Clanranald.

Moidertach had a number of his own scores to settle: his lands had been handed over to one of his kinsmen, Ranald Gallda, a protegé of

Lord Fraser of Lovat. When Moidertach returned in 1543, Ranald sought refuge with his benefactor Lovat, and Moidertach gathered together his allies the following spring. Joined by the MacIans, the Macdonalds of Glengarry, the Camerons, and Ranald Mor, chief of the Macdonalds of Keppoch, Moidertach led raids into Lovat territory and the neighbouring lands of the Grants. When Urquhart Castle fell to the rebels, it became clear to the Earl of Huntly that this was a direct challenge to the crown's authority. Huntly mustered the northern levy, including the Frasers of Lovat and Ranald Gallda, and marched against Moidertach; but the rebel proved elusive, withdrawing his men into the territory known as the 'Rough Bounds' between Loch Sunart and Loch Hourn. When Huntly conceded that his quarry had made good his escape and began the long haul home, Moidertach tracked him to the mouth of Glen Spean, keeping out of sight and awaiting an opportunity to attack. At Gloy (later called Nine Mile Water) Huntly split his force, sending the Frasers home as he made for Badenoch. Knowing that Lovat and Ranald had to pass by Loch Lochy in the Great Glen, Moidertach rapidly marched his men northwards and lay in wait for them there.

When Lovat reached Letterfinlay he got wind of the ambush ahead. He sent 50 men under Iain-Cleireach to a nearby pass to secure a safe line of retreat, then deployed his remaining clansmen to face the 500 Macdonalds and Camerons, who descended from the hills in seven companies based on their clan affiliations. The actual course of the battle on 3 July is clouded by legend, but it is reasonable to believe that the action commenced with an exchange of arrows, before a charge and counter-charge, followed by hand-to-hand fighting with claymore and axe. Folklore has elaborated the action somewhat, suggesting that the archery lasted some hours, during which time both sides shed their armour since the day was so hot – hence the battle's more romantic name of Blar-na-lein ('The Battle of the Shirts'); however, it is more likely that this is a corruption of Blar-na-Leana ('Field of the Swampy Meadow'). The fighting was merciless; another legend has the armourers from each side searching each other out in the mêlée and testing the quality of their work by striking each other until both succumbed to their injuries. The archers accompanied the charge, gathering up spent shafts and shooting at point-blank range into the throng. At some point Lovat attempted to withdraw, but his covering force had been wiped out, leaving him with no place to fall back to. The Frasers were annihilated; legend has it that only four of their number were left standing as night fell, and that only eight unwounded men of Moidertach's force were left to take their surrender. Both Lovat and Ranald were among the slain.

'Caterans' made up the bulk of the highland contingents; dressed in no more than shirt and an iron skull cap, they had few arms and little protection. (Alan Gault)

Huntly was incapable of dealing with this rebel; affairs of state called him south, and Moidertach was left safe in the natural stronghold of the Rough Bounds. In 1545 this self-appointed Captain of Glenranald sallied westwards in raids that took him back to the gates of Urquhart castle, and in September of that year John Moidertach simply ignored a summons to appear before parliament to face charges of high treason.

### Ancrum Moor, 1545

After the Treaty of Greenwich in 1543 it seemed that the union of Scotland and England was inevitable. However, the Francophiles and Catholics, under the queen-mother and Beaton, managed to persuade the fickle Arran that the infant Mary would be better off wedded to a French prince, and set about negating the treaty. In retaliation, Henry VIII sent Edmund Seymour, Earl of Hertford, to raze Edinburgh. In 1544 a seaborne expedition landed at Leith, secured the port and stormed the city walls; they set fire to the town, laid waste to the surrounding area, and marched back south almost unopposed.

At Ancrum Moor the Scots horse feigned a retreat that enticed the English cavalry to charge impetuously on to the waiting Scottish pikemen. The English fell back on to their own infantry, disordering them in the process; the Scottish cavalry picked their way through the mires on the enemy's flanks before charging home and forcing the English into flight. (Author's collection)

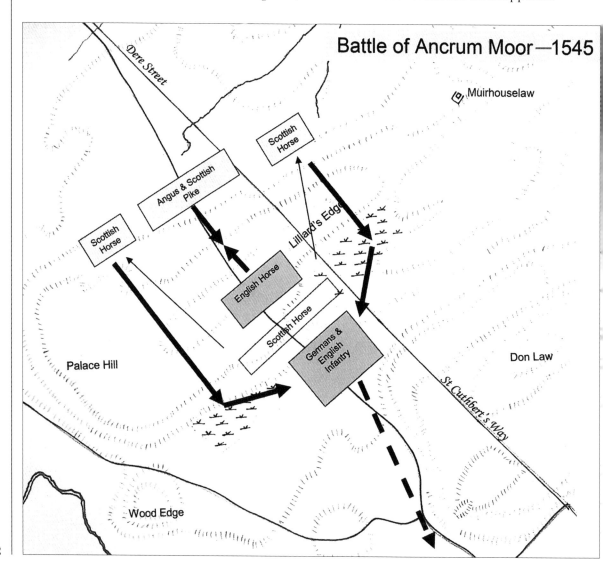

**Battle of Ancrum Moor—1545**

Dere Street

Muirhouselaw

Scottish Horse

Angus & Scottish Pike

Lillard's Edge

Scottish Horse

English Horse

Scottish Horse

Palace Hill

Germans & English Infantry

Don Law

St Cuthbert's Way

Wood Edge

The fury of this raid had unforeseen consequences: the pro-English faction in the Scottish parliament became disenchanted, and their mood was not improved by English forays along the borders. Raiders led by Sir Ralph Eure, Sir Brian Laiton and Sir George Bowes laid waste to Teviotdale, stripping the land of livestock and burning Kelso, Dryburgh and Jedburgh. Angus was particularly affronted, as much of the damage was caused on Douglas property; when the raiders desecrated the ancestral burial site in Melrose Abbey in January 1545 his previous loyalties were cast aside. According to the historian Lindsay of Pitscottie, Angus resolved to personally write his 'sasine' on the skins of Eure and Laiton with a sharp pen and bloody ink.

The monument for Sir Walter Scott outside St Giles on the Royal Mile in Edinburgh is adorned with scenes taken from his writings, many of which are based on the exploits of his ancestor, Sir Walter Scott of Buccleuch, who fought with distinction at Linlithgow, Melrose and Ancrum. (Author's collection)

Angus took 300 of his retinue from Edinburgh and headed south, gathering reinforcements on the way. He faced an English army of some 5,000 men including 3,000 German and Spanish mercenaries, 1,400 Border horse and some 700 Assured Scots, including Highlanders under Neill McNeill of Gigha. They had only just missed each other at Melrose, and the English were now marching back to the border. Despite being outnumbered almost five-to-one, the Scots were further incensed when they reached Broomhill to find that the garrison of the towerhouse had been burnt within its walls, including one old lady who had been seen burning to death on the ramparts. Days later the Scottish pickets clashed with English scouts, and Sir Norman Lesley of Rothes arrived with valuable reinforcements. By 17 February, Angus' scouts confirmed that the English were camped on Ancrum Moor some 5 miles outside Jedburgh; he led his force up to Peniel Heugh, a small hill from where he could look down on the raiders and they could see the Scottish outriders.

Angus had 700 lances from Fife under Arran, and a body of Reivers under the tireless Walter Scott of Buccleuch, but the majority of his men were pike-armed infantry with a smattering of harquebusiers. He was aware that such a force was no match for the English-led mercenaries in a pitched battle, so he employed a degree of Border guile in order to offset their advantage in numbers. The English, on spying the Scottish scouts on the hill, held a council of war; deceived by false reports that Scots had been deserting their colours the previous night, they concluded that Angus posed no serious threat. Sensing an easy victory, Eure mustered his men and had them advance on the enemy position. The Scots cavalry turned tail and disappeared over the brow of the hill along the Roman road of Dere Street; the English horse immediately spurred on in pursuit, not wanting to lose the opportunity of prisoners and booty. As they topped the rise they saw the Scottish horse disappearing over the next crest – and a solid wall of Scottish pikemen facing them in the shallow valley between. Too late to rein in their horses, and dazzled by the setting sun, the English cavalry threw themselves down on to the Scottish phalanx, only to be unhorsed by concealed pits and skewered on the waiting pikes. Those in the rear ranks veered off the road and found themselves bogged down in the surrounding marshland. The survivors retreated back over the hill, only to collide with their own infantry struggling up the far slope. The Landsknechts and Spanish mercenaries were thrown into disorder, as they were shot down by Scottish gunfire and blinded by the smoke and glare. Meanwhile the Scottish cavalry had picked their way through the marshes, disposed of the floundering English horsemen, and were now 'pricking' the flanks of the column. The Scots pikemen then advanced in good order, forcing the English back the way they had come; and finally, the 700 Assured Scots tore off their English insignia and turned on their paymasters.

The victory was complete; Scottish losses were minimal, while the English lost some 800 dead – including Eure and Laiton – and another thousand captured. Little is known of the fate of the countless fugitives who struggled back to the border, through an angry population keen to avenge the previous atrocities. The English were shocked by the defeat, and the militias along the border were readied to repel retaliatory raids; ultimately, however, the Scottish counter-raid was just another episode in a bloody and drawn-out series of border wars – it was never the Scottish intention to invade and hold English territory.

### Pinkie Cleugh, 1547

The devastating Leith/Edinburgh raid of 1544, and a less successful incursion to Kelso in 1545 in revenge for the defeat at Ancrum, had left Henry VIII's commander in the North – Edmund Seymour, Earl of Hertford and future Duke of Somerset – in no doubt that the Scots would never be persuaded to accept an English suitor for their queen's hand by intermittent raiding. He envisaged placing a permanent English fortification on the very doorstep of the Scottish capital, from which the garrison could protect and cajole a growing forum of 'assured' lairds. This 'Scottish Pale', similar to that around Dublin, would eventually become self-governing once the union of the crowns had been secured. The Pale would be set around a number of great artillery fortifications that could be resupplied by sea. Although this ambitious plan seemed to make sense on paper, King Henry would have none of it; he insisted on yet another major raid as a precursor to any long-term occupation.

Consequently, Somerset planned a two-pronged attack into Scotland. A feint in the west, led by Lord Wharton and accompanied by the exiled 4th Earl of Lennox, would strike up from Carlisle into Galloway, capturing castles suitable to house garrisons. The main thrust would be up the east coast, led by Somerset himself with some 18,000 men, under the Earl of Warwick and Lord Dacre as ward commanders. Crucially, this east coast force would be shadowed by a fleet of some 80 ships commanded by Lord Clinton, which would resupply the army on its march and be on hand to rescue them should the need arise.

In response, Arran struggled to raise the Scottish levy for a second time in the same year – he had already mustered 20,000 men to take Langholm in July. The 'fiery cross' was sent through the kingdom and the levy mustered at Fala, suitably positioned to prevent an English

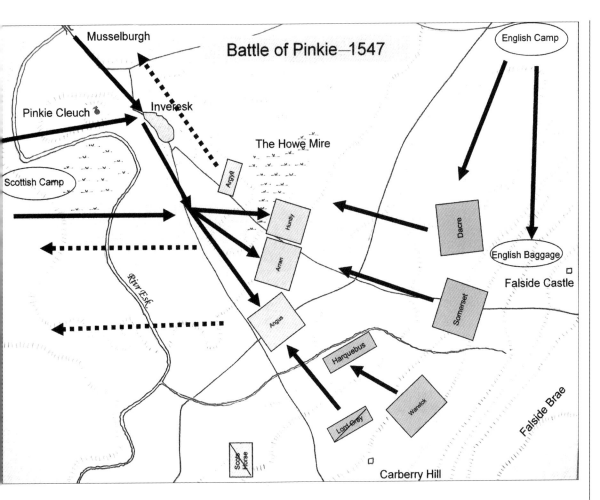

**Battle of Pinkie—1547**

Musselburgh

Pinkie Cleuch

Inveresk

The Howe Mire

Scottish Camp

Argyll

Huntly

Arran

Angus

River Esk

Harquebus

Lord Grey

Warwick

Scots Horse

Carberry Hill

English Camp

Dacre

English Baggage

Falside Castle

Somerset

Falside Brae

advance on the capital whichever way they approached. However, the muster took longer than anticipated, and the English advanced so rapidly along the coast that Arran missed golden opportunities to check them, first at the narrow defile of the Pease at Cockburnspath and then at Linton Bridge. As Somerset's men passed Hailes Castle, Arran scrambled his force into position along the west bank of the River Esk, the last practicable line of defence before Edinburgh. The Scottish host numbered in the region of 23,000 men, primarily armed with pikes, but also including some 4,000 Highlanders under the Earl of Argyll and 1,500 Border horse led by Lord Home. The pike were split into the traditional three wards, with Arran leading the 'main', Angus the 'vanguard' and Huntly the 'rearward'. All were experienced in fighting the English, if not in set-piece battles; 30 pieces of ordnance were dug in along the banks of the Esk, the coastal flank was protected from naval bombardment by an earth rampart, and the Scottish horse roamed the slopes of Falside Hill overlooking the advancing English columns. It was a formidable position.

Somerset approached rapidly along the coast, avoiding contact where he could, and resupplying from his ships over less than perfect landing sites. By the time he approached Musselburgh he was at the end of a tenuous supply chain, and could not afford to delay. On 9 September he despatched 1,000 light horse and 700 men-at-arms on to Falside Hill

At Pinkie, Arran abandoned his position west of the River Esk in an attempt to take the high ground of Falside Brae. However, his 'vanguard' under Angus was held up by a desperate cavalry charge by the English 'Bulleners' and men-at-arms. The following wards, hemmed in by the Howe Mire, struggled to face the enemy. Peppered by shot and arrow, the mass of pikemen became a sitting target; finally Scottish resolve gave way, and the rout began. (Author's collection)

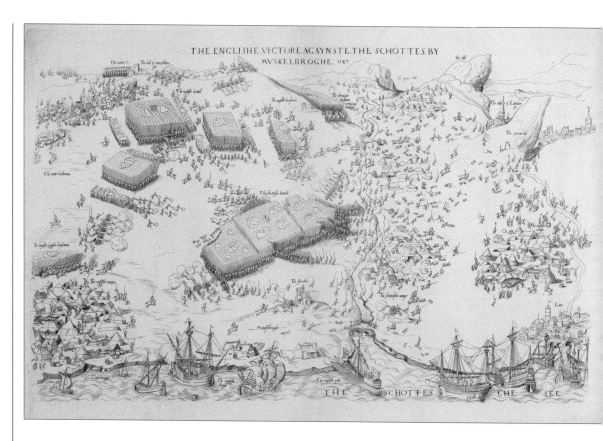

THE.ENGLISHE.VICTORE.ACAYNSTE.THE.SCHOTTES.BY
MVSKELBROGHE. 1547.

**This engraved image is the interpretation and combination of five preliminary sketches of Pinkie, reputedly drawn by 'John Ramsay, Gentyllman, without money' and now held in the Bodleian Library. The detail is extraordinary, and it seems plausible that it can only have been drawn by someone who was present at the battle. (© National Army Museum)**

under the command of Lord Grey of Wilton. Ahead of him were arrayed some 1,500 Scottish horse and – recalling the deployment at Ancrum – 700 concealed infantry; however, this time the English cavalry were kept under control. They allowed the Scots to approach and engage in the customary jeering and bragging before making off as if in rout; but this time the English launched their charge just as the Scots turned away, catching the horsemen in complete disorder. The rout carried on for some 3 miles, and the Scottish horse was decimated. Lord Home fell from the saddle, broke his collar bone and was evacuated to Edinburgh Castle; his son was captured; the Scots lost some 800 men to 100 English casualties, and those remaining available for the main battle had effectively lost the will to fight.

Saturday 10 September dawned bright, and Somerset made plans to assault the weak point of the Scottish line at Pinkie Cleugh, a small eminence on which stood Inveresk church – if this were captured then the English could enfilade the entire Scottish line west of the Esk. Clinton brought his ships to the anchorage just off Musselburgh to commence a bombardment of the Scottish defences, and the English wards began the march of a mile or so to their objective. Seeing the English on the move, and recognizing both the danger of losing the Cleugh and an opportunity to take the offensive with his pikemen, Arran had the Scots strike camp and surge across the Esk.

Somerset was at first taken aback by the rapid enemy advance, but quickly deployed his cavalry to stem the attack and give his infantry time to deploy before they could be overrun piecemeal. Once more he called for Lord Grey, and sent him forward with 1,800 heavy men-at-arms and

1,600 demilances. The cavalry plunged their mounts across the treacherous terrain of newly ploughed fields and threw themselves at the pike blocks, but to no avail; the Scots withstood the charges, and mockingly called upon the riders to try again. Grey himself was speared through the jaw; bloodied and blowing, the cavalry recoiled up Falside Brae, almost causing the English levy infantry to fall back with them.

However, this was to be the high-water mark of the Scottish advance. The lighter guns which had been manhandled forwards alongside the pike blocks were no match for the heavier English pieces, and the Highland archers, ordered to clear away the enemy's missile men, were suffering under the naval bombardment. The Scottish horse was in no fit state to lend a hand after its defeat the day before; in effect the Scottish pikemen were alone, awaiting the inevitable English resurgence. The English guns now began to tear great holes into the Scottish blocks, unopposed English harquebusiers fired into their wavering ranks from behind a ditch, and mounted Spanish harquebusiers caracoled freely out of the range of the lunging pikes, pouring deadly fire into the massed ranks. As the English levy prepared to charge home the Scots first wavered, and then fled.

The Highlanders left first, followed by Arran, taking to horseback at the first opportunity; Huntly and Angus attempted to stem the panic, but it was too late. The Scottish wards disintegrated into a fleeing mass of humanity before ever coming to blows with the English infantry. The English cavalry rallied, drove off their weak Scottish counterparts, and set off in pursuit. The rout lasted for some six hours, right into the suburbs of Dalkeith and Edinburgh; the Scots lost up to 6,000 dead, most of these during the rout, and 2,000 were taken prisoner. English losses amounted to no more than 800.

James Hamilton, 2nd Earl of Arran, proved both a gullible and an untrusting commander. He was among first to flee when the Scottish ranks broke at Pinkie in 1547; Patten notes that he 'took hastily to his horse that he might run foremost away.' (© Lennoxlove House Ltd. Licensor www.scran.ac.uk.)

# RECRUITMENT & ORGANIZATION

This period witnessed the largest Scottish armies ever to take the field, supported by impressive artillery trains and amply supplied with all the materials of war, despite operating in some of the most hostile terrain in Europe. The Scottish army that gathered at the beginning of the Flodden campaign was variously estimated at 30,000 to 40,000 men with 17 notable artillery pieces. James V's army prior to the debacle at Solway Moss in 1542 mustered 18,000 men at Fala, with another 10,000 in the vanguard on the border; and the Earl of Arran raised 23,000 with 30 pieces of artillery of various sizes for the campaign in 1547.

Two trusted methods were used to raise such numbers. The first was through the retinue system, by which troops were financed by the lairds as private armies, and in turn the lairds formed 'bonds of manrent' with the king; these ensured, amongst other things, that they would supply a military commitment calculated in man-days as and when the king called upon them. The troops were effectively the armed henchmen of the feuding lairds, well trained, well equipped and used to the rigours of campaign. However, their presence in a Scottish army very much depended on the whim of their laird, and the terms of their service were often vague and open to interpretation. Bands of marauding retinue troops led by dissident lairds outside the king's or regent's control had a destabilizing effect on their fragile powerbases. Incidents like the 'Cleanse the Causeway' fight in 1520, when the Douglases and Hamiltons fought a running street battle along the High Street of Edinburgh, were tantamount to gang warfare between feuding families. Fortunately, retinues were expensive to maintain and consequently few in number. The large numbers of men needed in times of national emergency were raised through a levy system.

In theory, every male between the ages of 16 and 60 was expected to join the army for 40 days in any one year. On the sounding of the common bell, blowing of hunting horns, the lighting of beacons or – in some more spectacular cases – the arrival of a burning cross carried by the king's messenger, the 'fencibles' (men capable of defending the burgh) were expected to muster on the local green or at the 'mercat cross'. They were to bring suitable arms, equipment and supplies for anything up to the full 40 days' service. Once the troops were sorted into their allotted companies, the rolls taken and absentees accounted for, they would march – or more often ride – to the army's muster point.

The muster put a very heavy strain on the populace. The roll for the Edinburgh muster in 1548 lists 736 merchants and their servants in three of the four burghs, and some 717 masters and servants from the craft guilds – a total of 1,453 out of a total population of around 10,000. Some burghs preferred to pay for 'wageours' or paid substitutes to make good the numbers; others supplied food, wagons and horses instead of men. The levy system's inherent weakness lay in the limitations it imposed on the length of service. The levy might be called out on more than one occasion during particularly frantic campaigning seasons, easily surpassing the 40-day limit – at which point they had every right to disband, especially if they felt their properties and families to be under threat back home.

Officials tried to compensate for the limitations of the system by calling on troops from burghs adjacent to the oncoming threat, thus minimizing the time it took to get men to the front line, or by staggering the call-up to allow the levy to rotate their tours. A muster of 1529 for an expedition to the Western Isles was cancelled, as the burgh's levy had to harvest their crops before they could be released; retinue men went instead. The levy system limited the army to a purely defensive strategy: it was virtually impossible to take the war far across the border, support protracted sieges or mount major expeditions abroad using levy troops. Even when they were on the defensive the Scots had to bring the enemy to decisive battle as quickly as they could, before their troops returned home.

Regular 'wappinschaws' (shows of weapons) were held to ensure that the levy was raised in good order and with speed. Acts of parliament specifying the regularity and the conditions of attendance were frequently issued throughout the period. The issue of the acts was usually in response to an impending campaign, or to a suspicion that local burghs were slacking in their duties. The acts listed, by financial standing, the arms and equipment each man was expected to bring with him; men of little or no wealth were excluded.

The local burgh sheriffs, bailiffs and aldermen were tasked with organizing the gathering. Not only were they responsible for enforcing the required standard of arms and armour, they were also to record the turnout, note absentees, and provide suitable refreshment for the gathering troops and onlookers (turnouts at wappinschaws were often boosted by the provision of ale and entertainment at public expense). Officials would also decide on who should captain the troops, and group the men into companies of anything between ten and 100 men. The opportunity was taken to drill the men in the use of their chosen weapons; however, there was seldom sufficient time to instil the discipline required to match the standards of a professional retinue. Those who failed to turn up, paraded with sub-standard equipment or sent unsuitable substitutes were fined. A full account of the muster would be sent back to the parliament, signed and sealed by a number of witnesses in order to prevent fraud. It would be these registers that were used when an army was gathered, to ensure that the turnout matched the expected roll. Late submission of the registers incurred stiff penalties.

Musters were not limited to the raising of armed men. Treasurer accounts refer to requests for manpower to build fortifications, support the movement of artillery and bring supplies to the army. These commitments seriously limited the number of man-days available to the crown for the actual campaigning.

Even in times of relative peace, life across the realm was a violent affair that required individuals to respond quickly to hostile activity. De la Brosse noted in 1543, during his time as an ambassador, that because of the divisions among the people of Scotland the population remained constantly under arms. The Reformation added to the apprehension within the country; he commented that even churchmen, friars and country people travelled in large companies armed with pikes, half-pikes, swords and bucklers. Inter-clan and family fighting was prevalent, and murder and 'stouthreif' (robbery with violence) were common. The weakness of government during the minorities of under-age monarchs,

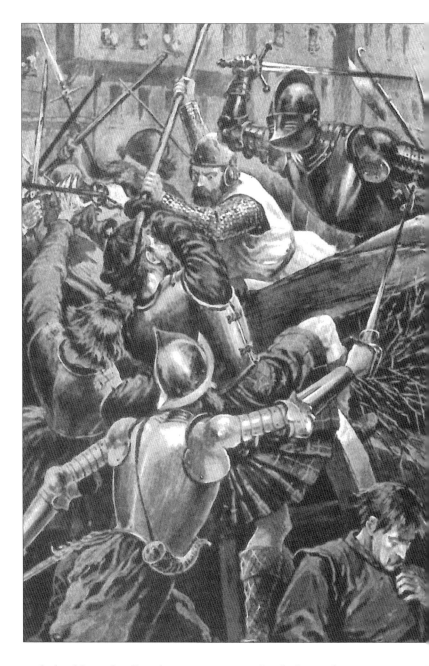

Another romantic Victorian study, of the battle along the High Street of Edinburgh which came to be known as 'Cleanse the Causey' (causeway) after the battle-cry of the victorious Douglases. The Hamiltons were funnelled into the street and hemmed in behind barricades before being butchered. Again, the dress and armour are fanciful.

and the bitter feuding between prospective heirs and regents, meant that the levy system was abused to raise armies in support of local rather than national causes, and the population soon became war-weary. James V's minority saw some of the bitterest feuding, culminating in the battles of Melrose and Linlithgow Bridge in 1526. Many of the combatants fought to settle old family scores rather than to decide the fate of the young king. The English and French manipulated the rifts between lairds in their own best interests; bribery, coercion and hostage-taking assured the loyalty of wavering Scots. Much of the populace in East Lothian during the 'Rough Wooing' of 1544–49 sided with the English, supplying food, refuge and safe passage for the garrison at Haddington, and thus prolonging the siege.

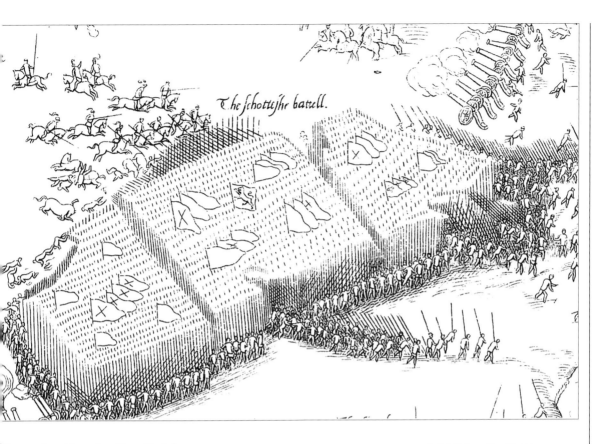

The schottishe battell.

## Organization in the field

Scottish armies were organized at the highest level along the accepted model of three 'battles', 'guards' or 'wards', traditionally called the 'rearguard', 'main' and 'vanguard'. However, this formation did not necessarily survive first contact with the enemy. At Flodden, James IV advanced on the English in either four or five battles, depending on the account consulted. The Earl of Lennox at Linlithgow Bridge was forced to attack with two battles, the third being dispersed by earlier actions and the survivors being absorbed into the remaining formations. The 'main' battle was usually led by the field commander in person, and the other two by his trusted lieutenants. While each battle would comprise a mix of troop types, it was common for the cavalry and artillery to be brigaded as independent bodies on the field. Wards were usually organized around the regional origins of the troops. This ensured that captains were familiar with one another, and inspired a regional loyalty; however, a drawback was that local differences such as religious persuasion, language and dress were emphasized, promoting mistrust and misunderstanding of comrades in the other wards.

Organization within the wards was an extension of that used for the wappinschaws. Albany's call to arms in 1523 was exceptional in detailing the need for the counties and sheriffdoms to be split up into equal areas, usually quarters. Each quarter was assigned a captain (a lord or earl), who in turn would split his ward by the same factor, usually by parish, or by 'other ways' by which they could 'ken his awn boundis and personnis quham he has to rais and bring furtht, governe and rule'. The captains would in turn nominate their subordinate officers.

A detail from the Pinkie engraving shows the three Scottish wards pushed together into one heaving mass by the fire from the English artillery on the brae and aboard the ships. The Scottish pike blocks can be seen ably fending off the English cavalry attacks. The Scots goaded their adversaries by calling *'Come here, hounds – Come here, tykes'.* (© National Army Museum)

In 1547 the French-employed master-gunner Strozzi took the castle of St Andrews within six weeks of arriving, after placing artillery on the tower of the cathedral and here at St Salvator's, now a part of St Andrews University. The Scots had failed to make an impression after 14 months of bombardment. (Author's collection)

The levy brought together at wappinschaws would be divided into suitably sized companies by weapon type, with their sergeants, 'whifflers' and 'ventemen' assigned by the burgesses. Although units of 20 men were recommended, it is doubtful that this could be adhered to when one considers the unreliable way in which the troops were called up. These units then reported to their regional captains at the muster, under their own banners and with their own supplies.

## TACTICS

The nature of warfare on the 16th century battlefield was rapidly changing from that of the previous century. The latest artillery technology introduced a whole new level of noise on to the battlefield (Flodden opened with the first artillery duel on English soil), the thick powdersmoke that hung over the guns on still days reduced visibility, and there was a marked increase in the effective killing range. It has also been argued that the introduction of gunpowder accelerated the demise of chivalry. The idea of warfare as being a noble combat between gentlemen – in as far as it ever existed – was seriously undermined by the introduction of firearms; unlike even massed archery, which demanded years of practice, firearms gave the barely-trained commoner the means to bring down a laird in full armour, and tactics changed accordingly.

On first review it would seem that little thought was given to tactics on a Renaissance Scottish battlefield. Massed blocks of levy pikemen seem to have been pitched into unco-ordinated advances on the enemy in desperate do-or-die charges, doomed to fail against any balanced and well-drilled opposition. But however clumsy these attacks may appear to be, they were in line with the most modern thinking of the time. The foremost military minds of the day were advocating the adoption of the classical style of infantry warfare, combining the models of Roman legionary swordsmen with Greek pike-armed phalanxes, and the theorists had recent practical examples to back up their conclusions. As James IV finalized his plans for the invasion of England in June 1513, news came of the crushing defeat of the French at Novara by the Swiss pikemen.

Scottish tactics kept abreast with these latest ideas from mainland Europe, the only limiting factor being the relatively fewer resources that could be called upon. The great reliance placed on the pike by Scottish armies was a legacy of the previous century. The Scots had been amongst the first to adopt the spear block or 'schiltron' as an effective tactical formation, and it had sporadic but notable success throughout the Wars of

Independence and in France against the English in the Hundred Years' War. This was long before the Swiss gave up their halberds in favour of the pike. If anything the Scots could be said to have imitated the Dutch, whose levy were successfully using pike blocks in the early 14th century. By the middle of the 15th century the spear was ordained by parliament to be between 5 to 6 ells long (15 ½ ft to 18 ½ ft) – a pike by any name. It was cheap, easy to source, and men could be given basic training in its use very quickly. Although we have few examples of the successful use of this weapon by the Scots in the late 1400s, there seems to be little difference between this formation and that of their Swiss contemporaries. It was the introduction of the 'Almayn' manner of fighting that radically changed Scottish tactics.

### 'In the Manner of Almayns'

In the 1520s Machiavelli explained in his *The Art of War* that the Swiss had to fight for their freedom against the Austrians who were a predominantly cavalry force; being a nation with few resources and a feudal levy system, the Swiss came up with the phalanx of pikes. (This must have struck a familiar chord with Scottish readers, as they reminisced on their previous victories over the English.) The Swiss recognized the pike block first and foremost as an offensive weapon, whose speed and momentum was the key to its success – so much so that the Swiss remained unburdened with heavy armour and did not use shields. There was no thought of deploying behind barricades, digging defensive pits, or standing on a hill awaiting the enemy onslaught. They advanced in 'battles' up to 6,000 strong, in echeloned lines so as to stagger the impact and to allow for tactical redeployment as the battle progressed, using the weight of numbers to drive

The battle of Novara, fought on 6th June 1513, was a timely reminder to the Scots preparing for Flodden of the devastating power of pikemen fighting 'in the manner of the Almayns'

BOTH **The mine and Castillion countermine at St Andrews are arguably the best-preserved pieces of Renaissance siege works in Europe. The countermine was the third to be started, and required rerouting on more than one occasion to ensure it met up with the Scottish mine. (Author's collection)**

through shallower enemy formations. They had few artillery pieces and even fewer bodies of cavalry. They had no formal command structure, instead depending on cantonal social structure to keep order throughout the ranks; collective resolve throughout the pike block was encouraged by local recruitment, and backed up with a strict disciplinary system. Perhaps most telling of all, they were accompanied by swarms of skirmishers armed with crossbows (latterly, harquebuses), and by 'forlorn hopes' armed with two-handed swords, employed to loosen and weaken the enemy's formations before the pikes hit home.

With one or two exceptions it appeared that this 'Almayn' style of fighting would ideally suit the Scottish host, and it was no surprise that James IV had set out to instil this new method in his troops before Flodden. Unfortunately for the Scots, it was the 'one or two exceptions' that would prove catastrophic. On the afternoon of 9 September 1513 at Flodden a contemporary source noted that the Scots 'came down [Branxton Hill] and met [the English] in good order after the Almayn manner without speaking a word'. But the Scots failed to imitate the Swiss in two particulars. Firstly, they deployed their heavily armoured leaders, including King James, in the front ranks, which in effect both slowed them down and subsequently left them leaderless after the first impact. Secondly, they failed to disrupt the English ranks by effective use of artillery or skirmishers, so when they themselves floundered along the burn at the foot of Branxton Hill they were set upon by a still organized and relatively unbloodied opposition.

Flodden extracted a high price for the failure to fully embrace the nuances of modern continental tactics, but it did not stop the Scots from trying again. In 1547, when the Earl of Arran left his fortified position along the Esk at Pinkie and advanced rapidly against the strung-out English army, he did so in the same 'Almayn' fashion – which was somewhat antiquated by then. This time the advance was so quick that observers compared the pace of the lightly armoured infantry to cavalry. They brought with them the smaller artillery pieces, cavalry support (albeit the reluctant and thinned-out Border horsemen), plus a number of Highland archers and probably a small scattering of harquebusiers to act as skirmishers. It would appear to have been been the textbook assault; but the result was far from perfect. They were faced by a relatively untested English army who had made up for their lack of heavy cavalry and harquebusiers by employing foreign mercenaries. In the end the Scottish pike blocks were first pinned down by English cavalry, then broken up by the murderous hail of small-arms, bow and artillery shot. Had the Scots pressed home their advantage with all the gusto of the Swiss, then the outcome at Pinkie could have been very different.

## Sieges

If Scottish tactics in the open field could be considered a brave yet flawed attempt to adopt the new military theories, then their record in conducting sieges during this period can only be classed as poor. Despite royal patronage for the development of impressive artillery, there was little hope of successfully concluding a siege in a single short campaigning season. Prolonged sieges were rare, as the Scots were constrained by the expense of sustaining such a concerted effort and the reluctance of the levy to stay around longer than their conscripted period. Notable successes at Ford, Etal and Norham during the Flodden campaign are overshadowed by the failure of Scottish-led forces to take Wark in 1523 and Tantallon in 1528. The protracted and botched attempts to take St Andrews in 1547 and Haddington and Broughty Ferry in 1549 were only brought to a successful conclusion by the intervention of the French. Where fortifications did succumb quickly, it was due to guile, bribery or negotiation rather than the employment of modern siege tactics (indeed, when writing to the Pope in 1546 the Earl of Arran put the fall of Dumbarton down to a miracle!)

## Raiding

The Scots did excel in the conduct of raids and counter-raids. They were such masters at launching lightning forays, creating havoc along the enemy's line of advance, cutting off supplies and repelling insurgents that Scots light horse were in demand across Europe for skirmishing, reconnaissance and raiding.

Haddon Rigg in 1542, Ancrum Moor in 1545 and 'the Tuesday Chase' at Linton in 1548 were all classic examples of small, well-equipped, highly-motivated bodies of troops using local knowledge to draw an unsuspecting enemy into well-prepared traps. The English of the Borders were no slouches in this form of warfare either, and the Scots certainly did not enjoy the run of the Marches – as the 'Ill Raid' in 1513 and Solway Moss in 1542 demonstrated. But ultimately the English withdrew from Scotland in 1550 because they could not sustain the effort required to garrison the Scottish Pale, and this was primarily due to the cost of resupplying the outposts in a territory that was home to significant numbers of skilled and hostile raiders.

### The Highlands

Highland tactics were determined by the rugged terrain over which the clansmen fought. The nature of warfare meant that the Highlanders preferred ambush and raid to pitched battles. Clan battles consisted of engagements of not more than a thousand combatants, exchanging volleys of arrows before charging headlong into the fray to settle the affair face to face; little quarter was given or expected.

Although this 'Highland charge' was fearsome in the confined rugged terrain of the glens, it had little impact in the battles fought in the Lothians and Borders. The Highland contingents' performance at Flodden and Pinkie was poor: in both, they fled before becoming fully engaged. The Highland troops that Lennox had with him at Linlithgow Bridge were the first to give way as the Douglas reinforcements arrived. Jean de Beaugué noted in 1548 that although the Highland troops made a spirited entry at the siege of Haddington by raiding the English trenches, as soon as the English artillery fired on them they 'shut their ears, and threw themselves on their bellies at each shot of the cannon.'

# EQUIPMENT & WEAPONS

### Armour

Throughout the latter half of the 15th century James IV had been building up an arms industry in Scotland to rival those on the continent. He had established 'harness' (armour) mills at Stirling, and contracted some of the finest armourers in Europe to work there. In addition he had bought armour 'off the shelves' in Italy and Germany, to equip his retinues with the best that his limited funds could buy. Merchant ships also returned with their holds filled with 'munition'-grade armour – breast- and backplates, faulds and tassets, sallets and iron 'skulls' – to ensure that his levy were as well equipped as he could afford. It was this equipment that kitted out the ranks of his pike blocks at Flodden.

Some 30 years later, when the Scottish infantry advanced at Pinkie observers noted a distinct change in appearance. The Scottish army had shed its heavy harness in favour of lighter, cheaper and more mobile protection (compare Plates A and G). This is understandable, considering the difficulty the Scottish noblemen faced when fleeing from Flodden: they were easily cut down by the lightly armoured English billmen as they tried to escape up hill in full armour. The Scots also realized that no measure of armour would protect the wearer from the effects of a harquebus ball.

The acts of Parliament detailing the type of equipment to be brought to the musters portray a similar picture. In 1540 gentlemen of more than £100 of rent were to be armed with full 'white' harness and suitable weapons; the middle orders were to have a jack of plates, a 'halcret' (half suit of plate armour with tassets) or brigandine, a gorget (neck protection), splints (arm armour), pans of mail for the knee, and gloves of plate or mail. The least a man was to bring was a jack of plates, halcret splints, and a sallet with gorget. Every man was to have a sword; other weapons were spears, pikes, light axes, halberds, bows and arrows crossbows, two-handed swords and 'culverins' (in this instance, handguns) No mention is made of the more specialized weapons – such as Jedwart staves and Lochaber axes – that had been acceptable at previous musters.

A full harness as worn at Flodden looked very similar to those worn in the previous century, being primarily based on an Italian style or the distinctively fluted 'Maximillian' armour, but as the 16th century progressed there developed a number of peculiar features which characterize the period. The foot protection evolved into a broad-toed sabaton, with greaves that extended down to the heel at the back. The lower line of the knee armour (poleyn) took on a straighter cut and it was reduced in size. Greaves and vambraces (lower leg and lower arm armour) were joined along the seam by spring-loaded studs, and the wing of the poleyn grew progressively smaller. Gauntlets that had been of mitten form now became individually fingered and had longer bell-shaped or pointed cuffs. The breastplate's waistline began to become more pointed and was lowered, in a precursor to the pronounced 'peascod' of the 1570s; it was also adorned with 'roping' along the edges, and the neck line was squared off in a style very reminiscent of the clothing underneath. Laminated tassets replaced single-plate faulds. The better harnesses were richly adorned with elaborate engraving and gilding.

The jack of plates, first mentioned in the 14th century, proved to be a light and cheap alternative to plate armour. It was a natural development from the padded aketon synonymous with the 14th century, and similar to the brigandine of the 15th century. It covered the torso from the neck to mid-thigh, and was fastened up the chest or along the seam under the arm by lacing, hooks-and-eyes or buckled staps; it was usually sleeveless, and could be worn over a mail shirt to provide an effective combination of protection. The jack consisted of layers of cloth, twill or linen, sometimes stuffed with rags, into which were stitched small iron plates, made from off-cuts or scrap armour, measuring between 1 and 2 inches square, and pierced in the centre for stitching. This gave the jack a quilted appearance. The outer covering was of leather, fustian, canvas or, in the more expensive versions, velvet, silk or satin. Sometimes more vulnerable points were reinforced by adding a fauld of mail or aprons of plate. According to William Patten, the Earl of Arran at Pinkie was 'adorned in a jack with splints on the arms and an apron of plate, all covered in purple velvet with an embroidered gold cross. The nails on the splints and apron were gilt'.

The term 'splints' was common in England to describe a combination of vambraces with a pauldron of three or four lames, fastened by rivets to a half upper-cannon, which in turn was fixed to the couter. Below this was a half lower-cannon finishing in a series of lames covering the back of the hand. Somewhat confusingly, 'splint armour' referred instead to narrow strips of metal attached to a fabric or leather backing or covering. The splints themselves were usually arranged longitudinally, and they, like the plates in a jack, were pierced for riveting or sewing to a backing or a covering, probably of leather. This splint armour was usually used to protect the arms but could be used on the legs and torso. In a similar manner, limbs were also given added protection by sewing or tying on additions such as interconnected bars,

This reproduction armour on display at the Flodden Museum is a good representation of the type of harness worn by the front ranks of the Scottish pike blocks; see Plate A. (Author's collection)

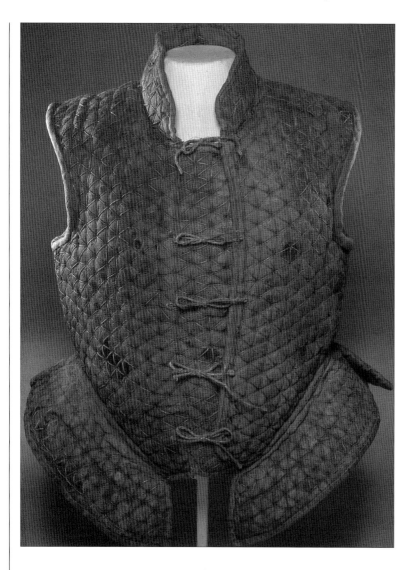

**The ubiquitous jack provided cheap, flexible and effective protection against anything except a harquebus ball (Trustees of the National Museums of Scotland)**

rings and small plates. Patten notably describes the Scots at Pinkie as using 'chains of latten' set along the sleeves and thighs (latten being an alloy of copper and calamine, distinguished from the darker and less costly 'brass', later known as bronze, which was made from an alloy of copper and tin.)

Helmets underwent a significant change in style during the early years of the 16th century. The sallet, popular in its many forms during the 15th century, developed a peak on the front, a flared neckpiece at the back and a comb across the crown; separate earpieces were added, buckling together under the chin. The result was the burgonet, the archetypal helmet for the Border Reivers. This was worn in combination with a 'buffe', a form of bevor with gorgets that protected the neck and jaw. The morion, a tall domed skull with a narrow rim and central comb, was also gaining in popularity, as it ensured good vision and hearing. The helmet was often padded to fit the owner, with a line of rivets securing the lining. The metalwork was sometimes blackened to prevent rusting.

The closed helmet for the cavalry man-at-arms developed from the sallet and bevor into one item, both elements being attached at the same point on the brow; when closed, the parts were held together by spring-loaded pins or hooks-and-studs. The protruding 'sparrow beak' was the most popular style of the period before it gave way to rounded visors in the later years. Closed helmets were often fitted with a number of gorget plates or mounted on a ringed collar. Helmets were sometimes adorned with plumes of ostrich feathers set in a holder on the rear at the base of the skull.

The Highland warriors favoured a simple bascinet-style helmet, often with a pronounced keel and occasionally with a knob-like crest; the sides were extended to cover the base of the neck or fitted with a mail aventail, and the face was sometimes protected by a nasal bar or oval boss. The majority of the levy and Highland 'caterans' (the poorest classes) could only afford a close-fitting metal skull cap or 'knapscall', often worn under a bonnet or other fabric covering. These were sometimes fitted with ear- and cheek-pieces.

# INFANTRY WEAPONS
## Polearms

The majority of the infantry were armed with a pike, a 16–18ft ash stave with a steel head about 10 to 12 inches long. The head of the pike was secured with 'langets', strips of steel riveted down the sides of the upper shaft to prevent the pikehead being lopped off in battle. Many of the staves were imported from Europe, and in particular the Netherlands, as the supply of suitable wood ran out in Scotland; the heads were made by local cutlers and blacksmiths.

In amongst the ward was a detachment of men armed with bills or halberds. These long-shafted weapons combined a cutting blade, thrusting spearhead and crushing spike into one multipurpose instrument. In theory these men acted as protectors for the banner-bearers, but they could be despatched to disrupt the flanks of the enemy and get amongst them once they had lost their order. Nevertheless, despite numerous mentions in the records for musters, there are no references to these men being used for anything other than adding to the weight of the pikemen during battles. There are, however, a number of accounts of small bodies of troops assembled for 'camisados' (night raids) and siege work giving up their cumbersome pikes for halberds or 'brown bills' – easier to wield and more effective in the confined spaces of fortifications and trenches. A halberd was often the weapon of choice kept at a man's home. There are references in the Edinburgh burgh records to burgesses and townsmen being allowed to keep halberds in their shops and premises, for self defence and to quell general lawlessness along the High Street. They were the preferred weapon for personal bodyguards and for escorts to the baggage and artillery trains. Halberd shafts, like pike staves, were imported, and there are accounts of a thriving halberd industry in Leith.

The craftsmen of Leith went on to put their name to another particular style of polearm in the early part of the century. The 'Leith axe' was described by the historian John Major as a 'double-edged axe' similar to a bardische or glaive, and 'was very similar to the French halberd but was a little longer and a more convenient weapon to fight with'. He goes on to say that these weapons, uniquely, were fitted with a hook at the end of the shaft. The term 'Leith' axe seems to have dropped out of use by the late 16th century, but the use of long-shafted weapons with heavy crescent-shaped blades that extended beyond the shaft, with or without hooks, continued into the 17th and 18th centuries.

Further south, the Borderers were arming themselves with the Jedwart stave. This fearsome weapon had a narrow 4ft-long blade mounted on a hardwood stave. The blades were only a few

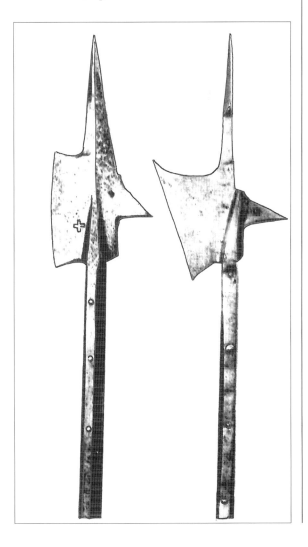

The halberd combined the benefits of a spearhead, an axeblade and the spike of a war-hammer into one weapon. The English used these to great effect against the Scots at Flodden once the latter had discarded their pikes and were relying on their swords and bucklers for close-in defence.

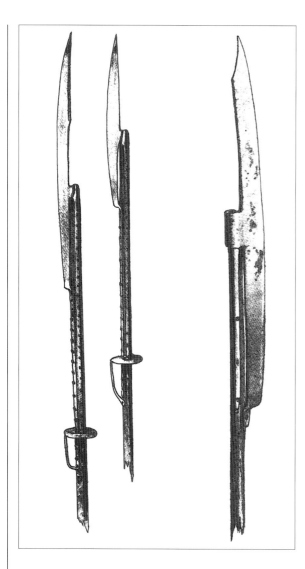

centimetres wide, and were double-edged beyond the stave. The stave itself was protected by langets, and rondels were fitted to stop the user's hands from slipping and to protect them from deflected blows sliding along the shaft. Jedwart staves seem to have had a patchy history, at times dropping out of the wappinschaw 'must have' list. This may have been due to the blade being too light to be effective against heavier armoured opposition. However, they remained a local favourite throughout the period, often appearing in the criminal records as the weapon brandished by the accused.

The 'Broggit' staff was also listed: similar to the English 'sprynckler', this shafted weapon was surmounted by a heavy iron head from which numerous spikes projected in all directions, and it was sometimes augmented with a spearhead to add a thrusting capability.

The Highlanders brought their own unique form of polearm to the battlefield, their weapon of choice being a long-shafted axe. By the early 16th century these weapons in their many forms were being called 'Lochaber axes'. John Major writes that they were single-edged and used by 'wild Scots of the north'. The tomb of Alexander Macleod, carved in 1528 at Rodel Church in Harris, clearly depicts this type of axe. The shaft is approximately 6ft long and designed to be used with two hands. When wielded by an expert these formidable weapons would have been capable of lopping off the heads of pike and pikeman alike.

Three examples of Jedwart staves, after the illustrations by John Drummond. These weapons were banned from wappinschaws for a time, as they were thought to be too light to be effective. However, they continued to be used throughout the century for personal and domestic protection. (Author's collection)

### Swords

The Scottish soldier could resort to his sword and buckler if he should lose his primary weapon. According to Machiavelli, the sword and buckler, in the right hands, could be devastating, and he recommended that half the troops be armed in this way. His theory was ably demonstrated by the Spanish at Ravenna, where they caused havoc in the Landsknecht pike blocks by darting in and out of the ragged columns, outflanking the plodding pikemen and bringing them down in their hundreds. Patten recounts that the Scottish pikemen at Pinkie performed in a similar role against the English cavalry. The majority of blades were imported, and there was never a royal workshop established for the manufacture of swordblades as there was for guns. Even so, there was a thriving cutlery trade, with no fewer than 25 tradesmen in Edinburgh alone in the early years of the century.

The acts of parliament issued to initiate wappinschaws in this period made little distinction as to regional preferences in weaponry; the requirements were so loosely defined that Borderers, Lowlanders and

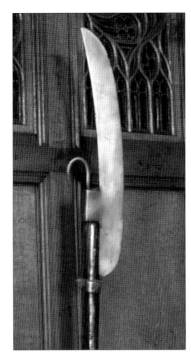

Two examples of Lochaber axes, now held in Edinburgh Castle. These items are probably early 17th century, but are representtive of those used in the early part of the previous century. (Author's collection)

Highlanders were all catered for, including in the latter case the infamous 'twa-handed sword'. The early years of the 16th century are credited with the development of the true 'claidheamh-mór' (claymore), which became the weapon of choice in the Western Highlands, and is widely depicted on contemporary gravestones. This weapon, anything between 4ft and 6ft in length, is thought to have had its origins in southern Germany; it was characterized by a round pommel, a large tang with a high collar, angled tapering quillons terminating in pierced quatrefoils, and langets extending from the hilt up the centre of the blade. The Lowland equivalent was distinguishable by straight quillons, but was otherwise the same. It is reasonable to believe that the men armed with these weapons could fulfil a role similar to the Landsknecht 'doppelsöldners', who preceded their own pikemen with the aim of disrupting enemy formations by cleaving off the pikeheads and exploiting gaps in the formation; however, there is no evidence for the deliberate employment of such tactics by the Scots on the battlefield.

## Bows

The use of archers by the Scots had never matched that of the more enthusiastic English, and the battles of the 15th century had proven time and again that the English archer was deadly against the packed ranks of Scottish pike. This is not to say that the Scots had no archers at all; a high proportion of the Scottish contingents sent to fight abroad consisted of archers, primarily recruited from the Borders, where they had seen at first hand the potential of the weapon. In the 1420s King James I had recognized the importance of training new archers, notably banning 'futbal' in favour of the men practising at the butts at least on every feast day. Merchants were required to bring bowstaves into the country as well as the traditional spear shafts. However, this fervour for the bow did not outlive that king's death, and soon the Scots returned to mustering with more traditional arms. The only notable legacy was the Garde Écossaise, the personal bodyguard to the King of France, who were primarily armed with the bow.

By the 16th century the majority of Scottish bowmen came from the Borders and the Highlands, where the use of the bow remained essential for hunting and dealing with troublesome neighbours. Despite both James IV and V being keen archers they made no attempt to establish permanent units of bowmen; when the Scottish army mustered in 1513 and 1547 it was the Highlanders who were asked to provide the archers – a role in which they failed to perform effectively in either campaign.

There was also a role for the crossbow in Scottish armies. While never employed en masse on the battlefield in this period, there remain a number of accounts of its use by garrisons and skirmishers. The financial records for the fitting-out of James V's fleet include crossbows and pavises. The Border horse retained in their already impressive arsenal of weaponry a lighter version of the crossbow called a 'latch'.

## Handguns

We have Patten to thank for the misconception that the Scots were slow in embracing the new firearms technology: his statement that 'hackbutters have they few or none' in his account of Pinkie has

A re-enactor demonstrates the use of a matchlock caliver during a display at Linlithgow Palace. The smoke and noise were new to the 16th century battlefield. (Author's collection)

frequently been argued as evidence to support such a claim. But Patten may have noted the absence of harquebusiers simply because it was exceptional rather than the rule. He also mentions in the same account a skirmish outside Preston Pans the day before Pinkie, in which Scottish harquebusiers played an important role and there is plenty more evidence showing that the Scots not only obtained these weapons but were happy to use them in combat throughout the period.

The French arms landed at Dumbarton in July 1513, some two months before Flodden included '400 arquebus and 600 hand culverins with their shot'; but these were not present at Flodden, as they were

(continued on page 41)

**FLODDEN, 1513**
1: Professional soldier, Montrose's retinue
2: French sergeant
3: Border horseman, Lord Home's contingent
4: William Graham, Earl of Montrose

A

**D'AUBIGNY'S ENTRY INTO PARIS, 1515**
1: Soldiers of the Scottish Guard
2: Robert Stuart, Seigneur d'Aubigny
3: Piper

B

**LINLITHGOW BRIDGE, 1526**
1: Sir James Hamilton of Finnart
2: Gunner
3: Pioneer
4: Harquebusier

C

ABOARD THE *MICHAEL* AT CARRICKFERGUS, 1513
1: James Hamilton, Earl of Arran
2: Seaman
3: Crossbowman

D

**BLAR-NA-LEINE, 1544**
1: Highland chieftain
2: Piper
3: Galloglas
4: Cateran

Graham Turner

**E**

**THE MARCH TO THE BORDER, 1523**

1: Lowland mounted infantryman
2: Baggage guard
3: Wagoner
4: Border horseman

F

PINKIE, 1547
1: Levy pikeman, Arran's ward
2: Banner-bearer, Clan Dury
3: Rattler

AFFLICTAE SPONSAE NE OBLIVISCARIS

G

1

2

3

4

H

recorded as being moved to Stirling three weeks after the battle. There is little physical evidence that the harquebus was used in any great numbers at the battle (although recent excavations of the site have found harquebus balls on Piper Hill), and there is no written account of the weapon being employed in 1513. This could be because their presence was unremarkable and required no particular acknowledgement, or because the wet weather led to their being left in the Scottish camp.

Mentions of the use of harquebuses increase as the years go by. When Lord Dacre wrote to Wolsey in 1522, concerning the massive build-up of the Scottish forces under Albany, he specifically warned that the Scots were armed with a thousand 'hagbusches' mounted on trestles and loaded on to carts in barrels, as well as a great number of handguns. He may have been exaggerating in order to support his case, but the force that did finally march on Wark in autumn 1523 was noted as being well provided with gunners and crossbowmen.

By 1535 parliament required gentry to be armed with 'hagbuts' and 'hagbuts of crochert' at the wappinschaws, but the Scottish arms industry was not capable of supplying good-quality firearms in sufficient numbers. Shipping merchants were charged with bringing home in each vessel two or more guns or the metal to make them, as well as powder and moulds, as payment to land their goods. The French were consistently called upon to provide guns and gunners to their Scottish allies.

The accounts clearly show the growth in the deployment of harquebusiers. The contemporary historian Lindsay of Pitscottie noted that Walter Lyndsey's vanguard at Haddon Rig had 2,000 spears, 500 bowmen and 500 gunners. A similar division of arms was employed in 1547 by the garrison at Dundee, where out of the 300 men raised, 200 were to be infantry of which half were to be armed with 'hagbuttis'. The stubborn garrison that held Kelso abbey in 1545 was primarily armed with harquebuses.

In 1548 the English garrison at Broughty Ferry were chased back into the fortifications by 1,000 'mounted' Scottish harquebusiers – a role in which the English were still using foreign mercenaries. The early 1500s also witnessed the development of the wheellock pistol. The first recorded use of a horse-pistol in action was at Haddington in 1548, when a Frenchman wounded an English man-at-arms before being cut down after being unable to reload his weapon in time. The horse-pistol or 'dag' was soon to become standard issue for Scots cavalry and Border horse.

## CAVALRY

The Scottish army had consistently failed to deploy an effective cavalry arm for the previous 200 years. The battle of Falkirk in 1296 marked the last use of heavily armed Scottish knights on horseback. Although the intervening years had witnessed the rise of 'chevauchées' (mounted raids) by the gentry, they had preferred to dismount to fight the set-piece battles. Flodden was no exception; when James IV chose to fight alongside his men in the pike block rather than remain mounted, this was not only a statement of his intent to fight to the death, but also a pragmatic decision – he recognized that his nobles were untrained for service as a heavy cavalry unit.

It was not that the Scots did not have enough horses: legislation required every man to own a horse as early as the 13th century, and by the 16th century there was a thriving export trade (legal or not) across the border. However, the horses were seldom of the right type for heavy cavalry, the majority being bred for everyday work around the farms and estates. There was little enthusiasm for keeping the larger destriers and hunters on the off-chance that one might have to go into battle mounted.

Both James IV and V recognized the deficiency in this arm, and attempted to improve the quality of horseflesh by importing heavier breeds from Denmark, Aragon and France. James IV set up stud farms at Doune, Dundee and Newark, and he used the Rapploch at Stirling to graze the stud in sight of his apartments in the castle. Linlithgow housed a fine set of stables where, according to accounts, James kept his 'bey gelding, black horse and his white nag'

Training horses for battle was a very time-consuming and costly business, and few lairds had the inclination to commit to such an expense. The gentry were certainly happy to ride to the battlefield on the finest horses they had, but without training in the tactics of charging home, knee to knee and lances levelled with their colleagues, when they got there they felt obliged to revert to the traditional method of fighting on foot. This would also ensure that their expensive mounts would be safely secured behind the lines, ready for a quick getaway or pursuit depending on the result of the engagement.

In complete contrast, the Scottish light horse was noted across Europe as an elite force. Their services were requested throughout the major campaigns of the period, including fighting for the English in France. The disputed lands of the Borders proved an ideal training ground for light cavalry tactics; for generations these badlands had been criss-crossed by raids and counter-raids as families pursued private feuds with or without the temporary excuse of Anglo-Scottish conflicts. The Border Reivers were entering their zenith in the early 16th century, and they provided the bulk of the light horse for both the Scottish and the English armies. The Reivers were raised in the saddle, taking part in the bloody border warfare from an early age and having to learn quickly the tactics of infiltration, raid, flight and ambush. They were mounted on swift, sure-footed, sturdy breeds such as 'cobs', 'hobbies' and 'galloways'; these were seldom groomed or stabled, often being turned out on to the pasture or moorland after the day's march. Estienne Perlin, who visiting Scotland in 1551, wrote of the Border horse:

> They are bold and gallant enough, but are not so well armed as the French, for they have very little well made, clean and polished armour, but use jackets of mail in exercising daily with the French, and have the custom of using little ambling nags and small horses; their lances are small and narrow, and they have scarce any large horses, and a few are brought to them, except from France.

These men would not think twice about staying in the saddle from dawn to dusk, sometimes covering the almost incredible distance of up to 60 miles a day, before mounting their raids in the dark of night. They carried all their supplies with them and usually lived off the land – a process that inevitably included looting and pillaging in enemy and friendly territory alike. Their loyalty was often questionable: Patten famously remarked that the English Border horse could be found talking with their counterparts on the Scottish side

> within less than their gad's [spear's] length asunder; and when they perceive they had been spied, they have begun to run at one another. But so apparently perlassant [unconvincingly] as the lookers on resembled their chasing, like the running at base in an uplandish town, where the match is made for a quart of good ale…They strike few strokes but by assent and appointment.

These light horsemen were often armed to the teeth, carrying an assortment of weapons including swords, small crossbows, bows, lances or 'pricker sticks', and Jedwart staves; by 1550 they could add a harquebus and a brace of wheellock pistols to their arsenal. It is said that

This detail from the Pinkie engraving shows the English baggage guard fending off an attack by the Scottish horse. Note that the baggage guard are primarily armed with halberds and that the train includes either spare draft oxen or 'beef on the hoof' for the army's rations.
(© National Army Museum)

The battle of Solway Moss in 1542 saw the complete collapse of the Scottish army under the constant 'pricking' of the English reivers. Note the variety of headgear, and the field signs or 'witters' used to distinguish friend from foe. (Painting by Richard Scollins, Keith Durham Collection. Licensor www.scran.ac.uk.)

the local lairds could raise a thousand well-armed riders within half an hour of sounding the alarm, or (as was more common in the Borders) the sighting of the 'Hot Trod' – a burning sod of turf carried through the district on a spearhead by a speeding horseman.

## ARTILLERY

The Stewart monarchs were keen exponents of artillery and took every opportunity to explore the development of gunpowder weapons. James II had lost his life at the siege of Roxburgh in 1460 after a gun he was inspecting blew up in his face. James III attempted to develop his father's interest by importing brass cannon, but he had little success before money ran out. James IV was more successful; by 1508 he had employed a number of French gunmakers, and appointed Robert Borthwick as master gunner. James had already used artillery to great effect when suppressing Highland lairds, and had honed his ability to move guns over great distances: in 1497 he had taken an artillery train including the great bombard 'Mons Meg' to the walls of Norham Castle.

Much of Blackness Castle on view today is the result of a major reconstruction between 1537 and 1543, which transformed it into one of strongest artillery fortifications of its age. The South Tower's walls were rebuilt to a thickness of 5.5m, and pierced in several places at ground level to allow artillery to fire to the south and south-east. (Author's collection)

The artillery train that went south in 1513 was one of the finest ever to leave the country. It consisted of five cannon or 'curtals' firing 60lb shot; two 'culverins' at 20lb (these guns were later to be named the 'Seven Sisters'); four 'culverins pickmoyane' firing 6–7lb shot, which had been taken out of the ship *Rose Galley*; and six 'culverins moyane' firing 5lb balls. The English noted after they had captured the guns that they were the finest they had ever seen, being gracefully shaped and of

The siege of Tantallon Castle in 1528 was a disaster for James V: his cannons failed to breach the walls of the Douglas stronghold due to shortage of gunpowder and shot, and his master-gunner Lord Borthwick was captured by Angus as they packed up to leave. (© Reproduced by kind permission of Historic Scotland)

'Mons Meg' was James IV's ultimate war machine; it saw action at Norham but, being left at Edinburgh, not during the 1513 campaign. Thereafter Meg was primarily used for the firing of royal salutes. (Author's collection)

a brilliant finish. The biggest guns were drawn by 36 oxen and manne by nine drivers, and 20 pioneers accompanied them with shovels, pick and mattocks to prepare the way and build the gun emplacements. Th smaller guns were pulled by 16 oxen and a horse, with four drivers an 10 pioneers. The cannon were hauled on primitive gun carriages c cradles, and 'cranes' were used to hoist the barrels on and off fc maintenance. 'Orkney butter' (a mixture of olive oil, wax and shee tallow) to grease the guns against rusting was packed into numerou kegs. Some of the shot was noted as being carried on 28 packhorse though an artillery of this size must obviously have required a great de more ammuniton than that. Not surprisingly, the artillery train require numerous wagons carrying all the paraphernalia for supporting th gunners and guns. The artillery left Edinburgh in three section between 18 and 20 August 1513, and the bigger guns were in position ; Norham on the 22nd after covering some 50 miles – a remarkable fea considering the poor state of the roads and the bad weather.

The development of Scottish artillery did not stop on the death of i main benefactor. In 1515 a new furnace was established in Edinburgl with Borthwick as the 'mastar meltar', a position he maintained unt 1531 (Borthwick's services came at a hefty price: treasury accounts sc his wage at £100 a year). He was succeeded by Piers of Rouen, who hel the post for the next ten years, ably assisted by Robert Hector. By 152 Albany had replaced the guns lost at Flodden, and took 28 cannon an four 'double cannon' to Wark, along with numerous smaller pieces c ordnance. Casting the guns was initially a slow process. The treasurer accounts of 1539–41 show numerous entries detailing the successft casting of new guns after weeks of work before they were finally proofec mounted, and in some cases elaborately decorated with the symbols of state. Demand again outstripped supply, and the Scots imported similar numbers of guns to those they had cast themselves.

The Scottish artillery may have looked impressive on the march, but it appears to have been poorly used on the battlefield. There has been much speculation as to why the Scottish artillery at Flodden was outperformed by the fewer and lighter English pieces. The inaccuracy and low rate of fire has been put down to the weather, poor positioning and inadequate skills (though heavier guns naturally took longer to serve than lighter pieces). What is clear is that the experienced naval gunners employed by the English outworked their Scots counterparts; the Scottish artillery notably failed to deliver on

**This replica breech-loading gun at Tantallon is typical of the numerous small pieces of artillery found in castles around the country. (Author's collection)**

Poetic licence has been used on the engraving of Pinkie, with the addition of double-barrelled guns to the Scottish left wing. Although there is evidence of such guns being used on the continent, none are reported at Pinkie. (© National Army Museum)

successive occasions throughout the period, both in the field and at sieges.

In 1528 the royal artillery from Edinburgh and Dunbar was deployed before Tantallon Castle to batter down the rebel Douglas fortress, but after 20 days of tepid bombardment the embarrassed king was forced to withdraw. To add insult to injury Archibald Douglas, Earl of Angus sortied out as the artillerists were dismantling the guns, killing the king's favourite, David Falconer, captain of the foot guard, and capturing Master-Gunner Borthwick.

In May 1546, the English-backed Castillians seized St Andrews Castle. The Scots under the Earl of Arran laid siege to it, and hauled up two large cannon under the names of 'Thrawn Mow' and 'Deaff Meg', as well as two 'bastards', two 'double falcons' and various smaller guns. There followed a protracted but ineffectual siege, rather hampered by the fact than Arran's son was being held inside the castle. By November the privy council called upon the French to send more artillery and, as importantly, skilled artillerists. Leo Strozzi was despatched, landing in Fife in July 1547. He repositioned guns in the towers of the adjacent college and abbey, as well as moving the remaining batteries to much closer range. It took him six weeks to prepare the positions, reduce the castle and force the garrison's surrender – a success that had eluded the Scots for the previous 14 months of bombardment..

In September of that year the same guns appeared along the banks of the Esk at inkie, well supplied and well protected; again, the number was impressive, with between 25 and 30 pieces dug in. Records state that the Scots deployed two cannon, one culverin moyane, one culverin bastard, one 'pas volent', and two other large pieces, as well as 20 small brass guns mounted on carts. Five hundred men were hired to serve them, to be led by a drummer and to rally under 'a painted banner of buckram'. However, when rran decided to launch his attack on the English army he effectively negated his advantage in guns, since he had to leave the bigger pieces entrenched on the west bank of the river. The gunners were then asked to manhandle their lighter pieces across the river and ploughed fields in order to support the pike blocks. All accounts suggest that they did this stoically, but could never make up for the imbalance in numbers in the final mêlée at the foot of Falside Hill.

Despite having debatably the finest guns in Europe the Scots continually failed to make best use of them. It was therefore understandable that when the siege of Haddington began in 1548 the Scots left the deployment of the artillery to their foreign allies; it was they who had to devise the taking of the new-style 'trace itallienne' fortress.

## Identification

The introduction of gunpowder to the 16th-century battlefield covered the terrain with walls of thick, acrid smoke; it was therefore vital that units could distinguish friend from foe both at a distance and in the mêlée.

There was a distinct difference between standards and banners. A standard was a long, narrow, tapering flag often denoting the headquarters of the laird or chief ; it did not necessarily signify his individual presence – that was the significance of his personal banner. Standards usually displayed the national saltire at the hoist (the end next to the pole). The remainder of the flag was horizontally divided into two or more bands of the owner's primary heraldic tinctures; his crest and heraldic badges were set out along the banner, separated by transverse ribands bearing his motto or slogan, and the standard was fringed with the alternating livery colours. The size of a standard was not fixed, but it was usually about 7ft deep at the hoist tapering to about 2ft at the fly end; the length varied according to the rank of its owner – anything from 12ft for knights and barons to 24ft for the king.

The statuette of the drummer from the fountain in Linlithgow Palace dates to around 1536, when the accommodation was restored by James Hamilton of Finnart. The hat of the figure is adorned with a rose, possibly as a tribute to the arms of the Earl of Lennox, whom Finnart had murdered at Linlithgow Bridge (Author's collection)

A banner was the personal flag of the laird, intended to locate the owner or his property. It showed only the coat of arms as it would have appeared on his shield, the design being conventionally placed on a square flag with the left side at the hoist.

The primary national device was the saltire, a white St Andrew's Cross on a light blue background, said to have been derived from a meteorological phenomenon observed before the battle of Athelstanesford in 832 A.D. The royal banner depicting the 'Lion Rampant' (Or, a lion rampant Gules armed and langued Azure, within a double tressure flory counter-flory Gules) was based on the arms of William I and first flown by his son Alexander II; it signified the king's presence on the field.

Banners showing religious iconography were used alongside the national flags. Patten singles out for comment a banner of 'The Kirkmen' which was flown at Pinkie, probably by the the Abbot of Dunfermline's retinue (see Plate G2). Images of Sts Andrew, Columba and Palladius would also have been common, as well as numerous other saints associated with places and clans; a banner bearing the image of St Margaret was flown at Flodden. That of the Garde Écossaise was traditionally some 6ft high, of red, white and green, with the image of St Michael adorned with the sun's rays.

At a lower level, each company would display its own colours – those of either their laird, town, or in some cases a craft guild. The cities and burghs adopted armorial ensigns as they gained more autonomy from the local lairds; these usually featured the laird's arms, local saints, historic events or landmarks. A medieval stone statue in the High Kirk of St Giles carries the oldest known arms of Edinburgh, the black triple tower on a rocky outcrop. Troops from Linlithgow were known to march under the sign of the 'Black Bitch', and those from Perth carried images of the 'Holy Lamb'. During a raid into Scotland in 1514 the Prior of Hexham's pennon was captured at Hornshole by the 'Hallwick Callants' – a contingent of unmarried men of that town who had survived Flodden – and was appropriated as the Hawick flag; a copy is still carried today at the annual common ridings.

Perhaps the most famous guild flag was that of the Incorporated Tradesmen of Edinburgh, who took their guidon to Flodden. James III had rewarded the guildsmen for their part in the protection of the city in 1482 by presenting them with a banner displaying a saltire, a thistle, an imperial crown and a hammer, as well as a lengthy inscription: *'Fear God and honour ye King with a long lyffe and prosperous reign and we shall ever pray to be faithful for ye defence of his sacred Majesty's royal person till death'*. The banner became known affectionately as the 'Blue Blanket' from its background colour. Many other guilds had similar banners, designed to be carried at community and religious ceremonies as well as leading the levy to war.

Pennons and guidons were assigned to lesser lairds and for cavalry units; these were flags similar in shape to standards. Up to 8ft long, they tapered to a round, often undivided fly end, and had a background of the livery colours of the owner's arms. The owner's crest or badge was usually shown in the hoist, and the motto or slogan was lettered horizontally – if at times somewhat haphazardly.

Retinues would have the additional advantage of a uniform of sorts, usually based on a combination of the livery colours of the household. Base coats, hose and caps might all be halved or quartered into the primary tinctures of the laird; alternatively the majority of the cloth would be coloured in the major tincture, and lined or trimmed with the minor. Coats often displayed household badges or symbols. The same colour schemes would appear in plumes and accoutrements, and were sometimes painted on to the armour.

Soldiers adorned themselves with various badges and field signs in order to avoid confusion in the mêlée. All troops on a national campaign would wear a saltire or simply the white cross of St Andrew

**The 'Blue Blanket' guidon carried by the members of the Incorporated Tradesmen of Edinburgh at Flodden appears in many Victorian images of the subject. (Author's collection)**

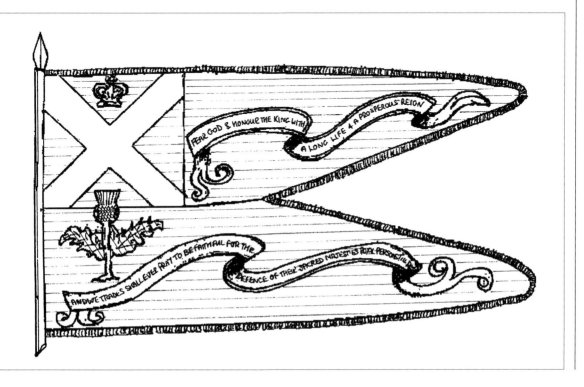

The pennon of David Boswell of Balmuto was reputedly taken by Sir William Norres at Pinkie. The field is primarily green with gold lettering, and supports the Balmuto coats of arms. (Author's collection)

on their armour, leading leg and / or arm.( It was claimed by Patten that many such badges worn by the fickle Borderers were so lightly stitched that a puff of wind might have blown them away.) In addition, and instead of the national colours during times of inter-family feuding, soldiers would wear family symbols such as the Douglas 'Bloody Heart', the Dury's gold crescent, or the 'Kerr Knot'. Hats and armour would be adorned with sprigs or flowers of the family plant, e.g. oak for the Hamiltons and Wallaces, club moss for the Munros, mistletoe for the Hays and laurel for the Grahams. Commanders would specify marks for the day, to be used for recognition; typically these field signs consisted of tying coloured rags around the arm, or fixing a sprig of a plant or other sign to the hat or helmet. Pitscottie noted that the Border horse at Flodden identified their allegiance by means of 'Ane wyspe [a twist of hay] wpoun ewerie speir heid to be ane signe and witter [mark] to thame that ewerie ane of them sould knawe ane wther' (see Plate A3).

Slogans were well-established war-cries, usually derived from the family name or the motto. The Hamiltons' call of 'Through, Through!' was met in response by 'A Douglas!', as Angus' men arrived at Linlithgow Bridge in 1526. Burgh militia used the town's or region's name, as did some of the clans: the Macfarlanes' cry at Pinkie and Flodden was 'Loch Sloy!'

## 'THE AULD ALLIANCE'

Perhaps the most tangible consequence of Franco-Scottish collaboration in the period was the prolific exchange of armed companies. The Scots had for many years sent contingents abroad to fight for the French king, most notably during the Hundred Years' War, where their presence was initially seen as an antidote to the English. Their reputation for hard living and hard fighting had seen their leaders well rewarded with estates in France – at one stage the Rhone valley was said to resemble a 'Little Scotland'. The Dauphin was so impressed by Scottish bravery and loyalty that he established the Garde Écossaise, a personal bodyguard of some hundred Scottish archers and men-at-arms. His generals included many Scots, including the Seigneur d'Aubigny, Beraud Stuart. Beraud had proven his worth in campaigns in Italy at the turn of the century, notably by defeating the great Gonsalvo de Cordoba at Seminara in 1495, for which he was richly rewarded. Beraud died in Corstorphine in 1508 while on his way to ratify the 'Auld Alliance' with James IV on behalf of Louis XII. His successor was Robert Stuart, who went on to surprise a papal force at Villa Franca and to take Brescia in 1510; Stuart's subsequent defence of that town for over a year made his reputation.

THE ARMES OF ALLIACE BETVIX THE DOLPHIN OF FRANCE AND MARIE QVENE OF SCOTLAND

Mary, Queen of Scots, was a week old when her father James V died in December 1542. Her future marriage became the focal point of competitive Scottish politics between pro-English and pro-French factions throughout her childhood. She eventually married the Dauphin Francis in 1558. (© National Library of Scotland. Licensor www.scran.ac.uk.)

Some 3,000 Frenchmen took part in the raid on Wark in October 1523, and left about 300 of their number dead when they withdrew; many more would die in storms at sea when the contingent was subsequently shipped back to France. (Alan Gault)

Contingents of Scottish troops can be found in all the major engagements during the Italian wars of the period. The Garde Écossaise took casualties at Fornovo ( 1495), at the second battle of Seminara (1503), at Ravenna (1512), at Marignano (1513) – after which the bells of Edinburgh were rung in celebration of the French victory – and at Pavia (1526). On surrendering his regency of Scotland in 1523, John Stuart, Duke of Albany went on to take Naples in the name of the French king in 1526. Scots troops notably stormed the walls of Landrecies (1543), and were fighting on both sides at the siege of Boulogne (1544). Undoubtedly many of the free companies that roamed Europe looking for employment had a fair smattering of Scots amongst them.

In return, the French presence in Scotland increased throughout the period. Albany's campaign of 1523 was headed by some 3,000 Frenchmen; and in May 1544, in response to the Earl of Hertford's devastating raid on Leith, a French force of some 2,500 landed at Dumbarton under the command of Gabriel Foucault, along with two large culverins and plenty of shot and powder. However, their subsequent raid on the border floundered in the mud within sight of Wark. This time the French retired to Haddington to recuperate, and the muster role there tells us something about their organization. The five bands each of some 20 retinue troops were each commanded by a captain, a lieutenant, an ensign and a *'commissionaire extraordinaire des guerres'*. They were accompanied by 23 men-at-arms, 1,259 *'hommes de querre a pied adventuriers francoys*', and 909 harquebusiers of whom 50 were mounted.

Much of this force had been sent home by February 1546, but their departure was somewhat premature: after the defeat at Pinkie the largest contingent of foreign troops despatched from France landed at Leith. This army of some 12,000 troops – 10,000 French, Italian and Landsknecht foot, 1,200 men-at-arms and 800 light horse – were sent to support the Scots effort to displace the English garrisons in Haddington, Broughty Ferry and Lauder. There followed at Haddington what was to become the longest siege in Scottish history, as the defenders and attackers fought themselves to a bloody stalemate in the fields of East Lothian. Plague, famine and spiralling cost in men and resources finally persuaded the English to withdrawal their beleaguered garrisons; that holding Lauder was the last to be called back across the border. The French, empowered by their victories, ensconced themselves in Leith and Dunbar – a permanent presence in the land they had fought hard to win back from the English.

## SELECT BIBLIOGRAPHY

Thomas Arnold, *The Renaissance at War* (Cassell & Co, London, 2001)

Caroline Bingham, *James V – King of Scots* (Collins, London, 1971)

Elizabeth Bonner, 'Continuing the Auld Alliance in the Sixteenth Century: Scots in France and French in Scotland', *The Scottish Soldier Abroad*, ed. Grant G. Simpson (John Donald Publishers Ltd, Edinburgh, 1992)

Jacques De La Brosse, 'An Account of the Affairs of Scotland in the Year 1543', *Two Missions of Jacques De La Brosse*, ed. Gadys Dickinson (University Press, Edinburgh, 1942)

David Caldwell, 'Having the Right Kit: Western Highlanders Fighting in Ireland', *The World of the Galloglass*, ed. Sean Duffy (Four Courts Press, Dublin, 2007)

David Caldwell, *Scotland's Wars and Warriors – Winning Against the Odds* (The Stationary Office, Edinburgh, 1998)

David Caldwell, *Scottish Weapons & Fortifications 1100–1800* (John Donald Publishers Ltd, 1981)

David Caldwell, 'The Battle of Pinkie', *Scotland and War AD79–1918*, ed. Norman Macdougall (John Donald Publishers, Edinburgh, 1991)

David Caldwell, 'The Use and Effect of Weapons: The Scottish Experience', *Review of Scottish Culture 4* (1988) pp.53–62

Jamie Cameron, *James V – The Personal Rule – 1528–1542* (Tuckwell Press, 1998)

George MacDonald Fraser, *The Steel Bonnets* (Harper Collins, London, 1971)

Tobias Capwell, *The Real Fighting Stuff – Arms and Armour at Glasgow Museums* (Glasgow City Council, 2007)

Jonathan Cooper, *The Heart and The Rose – the Battle of Linlithgow Bridge, 1526* (Partizan Press, 2004)

Jonathan Davies, *King's Ships: Henry VIII and the Birth of the Royal Navy*

*1509–47* (Partizan Press, 2004)

Gladys Dickinson, 'Some Notes on the Scottish Army in the first half of the Sixteenth Century', *The Scottish Historical Review xxxviii (1949)* pp.133–145

Christopher Gravett, *The Tudor Knight* (Osprey Publishing, Oxford, 2006)

Marcus Merriman, *The Rough Wooings – Mary Queen of Scots 1542–155* (Tuckwell Press, East Linton, 2000)

Norman Macdougall, 'The Greattest Scheip That Ewer Saillit in Inglande or France', *Scotland and War AD79–1918*, ed. Norman Macdougall (John Donald, Edinburgh, 1991)

Norman Macdougall, *James IV* (John Donald, Edinburgh, 2006)

Norman Macdougall, *The Antidote to the English – The Auld Alliance 1295–1560* (Tuckwell Press, 2001)

W. Mackay MacKenzie, *The Secret of Flodden* (Grant and Murray, Edinburgh, 1931)

Rosalind Marshall, *Mary of Guise* (National Museum of Scotland, Edinburgh, 2001)

Ewart Oakeshott, *European Weapons and Armour – From the Renaissance to the Industrial Revolution* ( Boydell Press, Woodbridge, 2000)

Raymond Campbell Paterson, *My Wound is Deep – A History of the Later Anglo-Scot Wars 1380–1560* (John Donald, Edinburgh, 1997)

Peter Reese, *Flodden – A Scottish Tragedy* (Birlinn Ltd, Edinburgh, 2003)

Gervase Phillips, *The Anglo Scot Wars 1513–1550* (Boydell Press, Woodbridge, 1999)

Gervase Phillips, 'In the Shadow of Flodden: Tactics Technology and Scottish Military Effectiveness 1513–1550', *The Scottish Historical Review, Volume LXXVII, 2: No. 204* (October 1998), pp.162 –183.

John Sadler, *Border Fury – England and Scotland at War 1296–1568* (Pearson Education Limited, Harlow, 2005)

Matthew Strickland & Robert Hardy, *The Great Warbow* ( Sutton Publishing, Stroud, 2005)

Stephen Wood, *The Auld Alliance – Scotland and France, The Military Connection* (Mainstream Publishing, Edinburgh, 1989)

# PLATE COMMENTARIES

## A: FLODDEN, 1513

### A1: Professional soldier, Montrose's retinue

This returned veteran of France's Italian war, armed with a half-pike, wears half armour and a 'casquetel' helmet – the forerunner of the burgonet. He carries a pavise as defence against the anticipated English bowmen; the Scottish front ranks were so well protected that English observers noted that their desultory arrow-storm had little effect. Although supported by a diagonal strap – 'guige' – the pavise was cumbersome to carry, and was most likely discarded as the pike block disintegrated under the English counter-attack. The front is painted in halves of yellow and black, with the saltire and – mostly hidden at this angle – the Montrose scallop-shell badge.

### A2: French sergeant

The French provided guns and powder to the Scottish king prior to the 1513 campaign, as well as 50 men-at-arms, and 40 captains to train the Scots in using the pike. This sergeant wears an old-fashioned visored sallet, adorned with a yellow and black scarf to associate him with the Montrose retinue. The heavy wool 'base coat' worn over his cheap 'Almayne rivet' munition armour bears the white cross of St Denis that identifies him as being in French service, and a saltire has been attached to the left breast to aid recognition. He carries

an 8ft halberd, primarily used to shepherd the ranks into position. All these French advisors were reported killed during the battle, some reputedly murdered by the disillusioned Scots.

### A3: Border horseman, Lord Home's contingent

This rider is based on the figure in John Skelton's *Ballade of the Scottyshe Kynge*. The Borderers dismounted for the fighting at Flodden and joined the pike blocks. He wears a simple skull cap with ear protection, a brigandine with a scalloped hem over a short-sleeved mail shirt, and plate upper leg defences. His 8ft spear with langets is adorned with a twist of hay or straw as a 'witter' or field sign. His mare is a typical nag or hobbler, about 13 hands high, which places her in the modern-day range for a pony; the classic Fell or Galloway had good shoulders, a short back, heavy quarters, and short thick legs, well suited to the harsh terrain of the Borders.

### A4: William Graham, Earl of Montrose

This reconstruction shows the typical armour and equipment of a wealthy Scottish laird who stood in the front ranks of the pike blocks. The armour is based on a German harness of c.1510 now in the Wallace Collection, with a close-fitting German armet with cheek pieces hinged behind the ears. The breastplate has been painted with the white cross of St Andrews. A base skirt of fine kersey is worn at the waist in yellow with a black trim adorned with yellow scallop shells, the heraldic symbol of the Montrose household. It is secured at the waist by a belt just under the cuirass, covers the tassets, taces and loin guard, and hangs to just above the knee cops. The earl, like his king, has decided to dismount and carry a pike into action.

## B: D'AUBIGNY'S ENTRY INTO PARIS, 1515

### B1: Soldiers of the Scottish Guard

The scene depicts the entry of the French monarch, Francis I, into Paris for his coronation in January 1515. Before him marched 24 Scottish 'archers' of his personal bodyguard, led by their captain Robert Stuart, Seigneur d'Aubigny. The Scots had provided the manpower for the guard since the beginning of the 15th century, and their loyalty and valour had been unsurpassed. A contemporary account of the parade details the guard as being 'armed with halberds, wearing white cloth jerkins with gold borders, white hose, and helmets with white plumes' – the latter shown at right, under the tabbed bonnet. The knee-length jerkin has a snug-fitting top with half sleeves, and a gored skirt lined with linen; it is trimmed with gold, with fleurs-de-lys worked into the ribbon. Jerkins were made of fine materials such as brocades, silks, velvets, or in this case finest wool. The jerkin is adorned with a crowned silver salamander, Francis's heraldic device.

John Skelton's *A ballade of the Scottyshe King* is illustrated with a woodcut depicting what is thought to be a Border horseman wearing a jack, a mail coat, and an iron skull cap with unusual ear protection; see Plate A3. (Author's collection)

Shipbuilding was an obsession for James IV; in total he had built, commissioned or bought 38 ships for his navy throughout his reign – compared with Scotland's population, one of the largest navies *per capita* in the world. In August 1506 the first accounts were raised for the greatest ship of them all: built at Newhaven at a cost of some £30,000 (Scots) , the *Great Michael* – as she came to be known – was briefly the biggest vessel afloat, and was a watershed in the design of fighting ships. She was probably about 180ft long with a displacement of 1,000 tons, and had an armament of 24 bronze cannon and 3 basilisks. Launched on 12 October 1511, she took another year to fit out. Her ongoing cost was to be her eventual undoing – it cost £500 (Scots) a month simply to pay the wages of the 300-man crew, and victualling added another £168 a month – this, at a time when the national annual revenue was

approximately £35,000 (Scots). James always intended to hire the ship out into French service and transfer the running costs to his ally's accounts, but after his death at Flodden the Scottish treasurery was forced to sell the ship to the French outright for £18,000 (Scots) in order to balance the books.

### B2: Robert Stuart, 4th Seigneur d' Aubigny

This figure is based on frescoes painted in c.1520 at the Chateau de la Verrerie, Aubigny-sur-Nere, and depicts d'Aubigny in full ceremonial harness and trappings. The sallet, bevor and gauntlets are of 15th-century styles, while the leg-armour is more modern. The loose-fitting heraldic tabard is quartered with the Stuart coat of arms, yellow with bands of blue and white chequers, and the French arms of three gold fleurs-de-lys on blue. The central shield shows the Lennox arms of a red saltire on white with red roses, and the borders are adorned with gold Aubigny buckle symbols. Stuart – who seems to wear the collar of the Order of St Michel – went on to lead the Guard through the campaigns in Italy, notably at the battles of Agnadel and Marignano (1515).

### B3: Piper

Scottish troops fought across Europe in various mercenary units throughout the early 16th century, and took their pipes with them on campaign. This figure is based on Albrecht Dürer's print dated 1514; drawn during his time in Nuremberg and probably depicting a local *Sackpfeifer*, it may typify the type of costume and arms adopted by the Scots while serving on the continent.

## C: LINLITHGOW BRIDGE, 1526
### C1: Sir James Hamilton of Finnart

The 'Bastard of Arran' was the illegitimate son of James Hamilton, 1st Earl of Arran, by Mary Boyd of Bonshaw. Being a key member of the Hamilton family, and second cousin to King James V, he became a prominent member of Scottish society; his fall from grace and execution in 1540 was primarily due to his having murdered the Earl of Lennox, the king's favoured uncle, during the battle at the bridge 14 years previously. His fur-lined velvet bonnet bears the Hamilton badge of an oaktree growing up through a saw. Hidden at this angle, on the right sleeve of the fine velvet base coat worn over his harness is a large white silk cinquefoil badge. He wears the harness of a man-at-arms, but has discarded his lower leg armour in favour of more comfortable riding boots for touring the works. His weapons are a fine Italian sword and a rondel dagger.

### C2: Gunner

The appointment of master gunner to the king was held by Lord Borthwick at the time of the battle; here we see a senior member of his retinue advising on the positioning of the guns – that shown behind the line of gabions is a heavy culverin firing 20lb shot. Over his linen shirt he is wearing a retinue coat in the Borthwick colours of white and black; his simple black velvet skull cap bears a cloth badge showing the Borthwick coat of arms – three black cinquefoils on white. His sidearms are the ubiquitous 'bollock' dagger above his purse, and a broad-bladed hangar with a single knuckle guard. He carries the plumb bob and protractor used to measure the elevation of the guns.

### C3: Pioneer

This labourer has stripped down for strenuous work. He wears a linen shirt with neck and cuffs gathered with strings, and the lace-on sleeves have been removed from his doublet to free up his arms. The sleeves were attached through rows of holes around the armholes by 'points', similar to those

hich attach his slashed woollen hose – note the long shirt-
il showing through the slashes. His cap is adorned with a
d-on-white 'Douglas heart' badge. His wooden spade is
inforced with iron sheathing at the blade, and his pick has
e spatulate mattock point.

## 4: Harquebusier

his handgunner is preparing his match (sisal cord soaked in
altpetre) before going on picket duty. He wears a thick
oollen cap over his iron 'knapscall'; it bears a pewter badge
St Barbara, the patron saint of gunners, and a sprig of oak,
e plant badge of the Hamiltons. The jerkin worn under his
eap breastplate and over the jack is made of white linen
immed with red; his allegiance is displayed in the form of a
oth badge of the Hamiltons – three white cinquefoils on red
the left upper arm. His primary weapon is an early
erman matchlock harquebus; the leather bullet pouch, and
s dagger, are hidden here beyond his right hip, and he
rries powder in a slung cow's-horn plugged with wood.

## : ABOARD THE 'MICHAEL' AT
ARRICKFERGUS, 1513

July 1513, King James despatched the Earl of Arran on
ard the Michael with his new fleet of 26 ships to France via
e Irish Sea. Arran broke his journey to assist the Irish rebels
der Hugh O'Donnell of Tyrconnell in bombarding the
nglish stronghold of Carrickfergus; the fleet successfully
urnt the town, but failed to take the castle. Arran then put
to Ayr to resupply before proceeding south to France. This
effectual and costly sideshow meant that the opportunity
bottle up the English in Calais was lost .

### D1: James Hamilton, Earl of Arran

The earl directs the fire wearing his finest harness and
weapons; he has removed his 'sparrow-beak' armet helmet
to allow him to convey orders more readily, and his sabatons
to allow a surer grip on deck. The admiral's whistle that
hangs around his neck on a silver chain was not only a
badge of office but was also used to convey orders and
encourage the troops. His base skirt of red velvet is trimmed
with the cinquefoils of the Hamilton family.

### D2: Seaman

The attire of the sailor manning the swivel gun is based on
items of clothing recovered from the Mary Rose. The doublet
of tanned and tarred hide is loose-fitting to allow easy
movement; it is decoratively slashed and 'pinked' on the
torso, which adds flexibility to the leather. A heavy, full-
sleeved canvas shirt is worn underneath, and a white cloth
tied around his arm identifies him as a Scot. The baggy
canvas breeches or slops have also been tarred for
waterproofing; he wears footless socks or 'scroggers' for

A spirited impression of a sea-battle of the period. The
Scottish admiral Andrew Barton's ship the Lion,
accompanied by the pinnace Jenny Pirwin, was hunted
down by Sir Thomas and Edward Howard off the Downs in
1511. Barton reputedly died still blowing on his admiral's
whistle in order to encourage his men. Both ships were
captured, and in English service the Lion was renamed the
Great Harry.

LEFT **An enhanced representation of the Rodel effigy showing a highland laird in his full armour. (Author's collection)**

RIGHT **This second effigy depicts a Western Isles laird out hunting; the enhanced drawing shows clearly the peculiar high-crested helmet and the aketon beneath the mail hauberk – see Plate E1. (Author's collection)**

extra warmth, but goes barefooted for extra grip on the wet wooden decks. He wears a simple wooden rosary around his neck, and carries the match for firing the swivel in a linstock with a carved head. At his feet are removable breech chambers loaded with powder and hailshot, and a wedge and mallet for securing them to the barrel.

### D3: Crossbowman

The crossbow remained a potent shipboard weapon throughout the 16th century. This man, kneeling under cover of the bulwark while spanning his bow with a cranequin, is partly based on a detailed study in Hans Holbein's 'Martyrdom of St Sebastian', c.1516, and partly on items in the Kelvingrove Museum, Glasgow. This type of sallet was relatively out-dated by 1511, but a 15th-century example now in the Kelvingrove collections shows signs of later enlargement of the face-opening, which would give a crossbowman good all-round vision and adequate protection. The breastplate worn over the puffed and slashed doublet woiuld be secured by straps crossed at the back, passing from each shoulder to the opposite hip. The sidearm, obscured here, might be a broad-bladed falchion.

### E: BLAR-NA-LEINE, 1544

The historian John Major gives a detailed description of the dress worn by the Highlanders in 1521:

*'From the middle of the thigh to the foot they have no covering for the leg, clothing themselves with a mantle instead of an upper garment, and a shirt dyed with saffron. They always carry a bow and arrows and a very broad sword with a small halbert, a large dagger sharpened on one side only, but very sharp, under the belt. In time of war they cover their whole body with a shirt of mail of iron rings and fight in that. The common people of the wild Scots rush into battle having their bodies clothed with a linen garment sewed together in patchwork and daubed with pitch, with a covering of deerskin.'*

### E1: Highland chieftain

This figure is based on the effigy of William Macleod found in Rodel, Harris and dated to around 1539. The effigy depicts the chieftain wearing a bascinet with a very pronounced keel and a knob terminal; the sides of the helmet extend to the base of the neck, and over the centre of the face opening a nasal bar terminates in an oval boss. The outer garments have the look of a robe and hood on the effigy, but they are

The Scottish camp on the Pinkie engraving, showing the types of tents and equipment used; see Plate G. Patten says of the soldiers' tents: *'They were tentacles rather cabins and couches of their soldiers which they had framed of four sticks about an ell long a piece. Where of two fastened together at one end aloft and the two ends beneath stuck in the ground an ell asunder standing in the manner like the bow of a sow's yoke. Over two such bows one as it were at their head the other at their feet they stretched a sheet down on both sides whereby their cabins came roofed like a ridge but scant shut at both ends ... They stuffed them so thick with straw that as weather was not very cold when they were couched they were as warm as if they had been wrapped in horsedung.'* (© National Army Museum)

## F: THE MARCH TO THE BORDER, 1523

Each man was expected to bring up to 40 days' supplies with him on his horse or on carts; once these ran out or were lost the army tended to disintegrate. The baggage trains stretched for miles along the line of march over unsurfaced roads, which became muddy and rutted in bad weather.

### F1: Lowland mounted infantryman

The majority of troops brought their own mounts on campaign, but many were no more than pack animals for the carriage of food and fodder. This rider is suitably dressed against the bad weather, and carries a Jedwart stave as his primary weapon; note the disc and knuckle bow on the shaft to protect his hand in battle.

### F2: Baggage guard

This young man assigned to protect the baggage train on the march typifies the recycling of armour that was commonplace among the burgh armouries. The majority of his equipment dates back some 50 years, and has seen better days – the Milanese gauntlets, plackart, sword, and the blackened sallet slung behind his hip are all late 15th century. The saltire has been sewn to both his gambeson and one thigh of his hose.

### F3: Wagoner

In addition to – or in place of – a levy of men, the burghs might provide carts and draft animals; these would be laden with pikes, barrels of powder and shot, and kegs of salted meat, bread and ale. They would be in the charge of wagon drivers, wearing everyday civilian outdoor clothing.

### F4: Border horseman

This Reiver has attached himself to the column in order to protect it against English 'prickers'. He wears a steel skull cap over a linen coif and under a woollen bonnet, with the saltire loosely tacked to it. His knee-length hooded cloak falls to cover the hindquarters of his pony; under it he wears a roll-topped cuirass of breast- and backplate, over a padded jack. A yellow identification rag is just visible tied around his left arm; hidden here are thigh-length riding boots with prick spurs. This typically heavily armed horseman

---

fact a mail hauberk with a separate 'standard' with a stiff raised collar. Under this he wears a padded shin-length keton covered in soft leather, the hem protruding below the mail. The 'claymore' was usually housed in the scabbard hung across the back and was drawn over the left shoulder.

**2: Piper**
This boy is based on a picture of a young musician found in a missal from the Abbey of Rossgall, Co. Kildare. He wears a 'leine' (shirt) of saffron yellow gathered at the waist with a belt, and with sleeves slightly flared at the wrist. An antiquated sword is held in a sheath tooled with a simple cross-hatch pattern, with an iron chape and throat.

**3: Galloglas**
This term originated in Ireland, for a foreign soldier, and came to be associated with those from their usual place of origin, the Western Isles. This figure too is mainly based on an effigy, this time from Kilminian, Isle of Mull. Although the keton suggests a 15th century date, the claymore shown in the effigy seems to date it to the early 16th. The helmet is a bascinet with the skull drawn up into a high, angular peak. The quilted coat, described in contemporary sources as *anneus lineus*, is made of tubes of linen stuffed with cloth or horsehair and daubed with waterproof pitch. It falls to just above the knee, and is gathered at the waist with a belt. The sidearms are an old hand-and-a-half sword with angled quillons, and a 'bollock' dagger; the axe has a 6ft ash shaft and a head of a typical West Coast design.

**4: Cateran**
This poorest class of fighting man made up the bulk of the Highland contingents. He has only the most basic equipment: an iron skullcap, an 8ft spear, a small target for self-defence, and a hatchet thrust in his belt. The mantle is the forerunner of the plaid, and shows woven strips of contrasting colours – in this case, various hews of brown; it is held at the shoulder by an iron brooch.

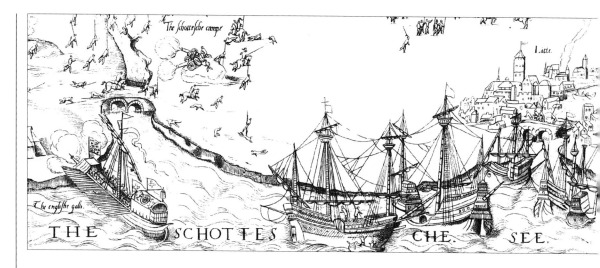

The detail of the Pinkie engraving showing the English ships off Leith. The Scottish left wing came under withering bombardment from the fleet during the initial stages of the battle. (© National Army Museum)

carries a 8ft border lance, sword and dagger, with a target – and probably a 'latch' and a quiver of bolts – slung from his saddle, together with a forage sack and bedroll. By the middle of the century he would have added a brace of wheellock pistols to his armoury.

## G: PINKIE, 1547

William Patten has left us a vivid description of the Scottish pikemen who fought at Pinkie:

*'They came to the field all well furnished withand skull, dagger, buckler, and swords all notably broad and thin, of exceedingly good temper and universally so made to slice, that I never saw any so good, so think I it hard to devise a better. Hereto every man his pike; and a great keche [scarf] wrapped twice or thrice about his neck; no for cold but for [against] cutting... To these another and not the meanest matter was that their armour among them so little differed and their apparel was so base and beggarly wherein the Lurdein was, in an manner, all one with the lord; and the Lound with the Laird all clad alike with jacks covered in white leather; doublets of the same or of Fustian and the most commonly all white hosen. Not one with either chain brooch ring or garment of silk that I could see; unless chains of latten drawn four or five times along the thighs of their hosen, and doublet sleeves [to protect against] cutting: and of that I saw many. This vileness of port [simplicity of gear] was the cause that so many of their great men and gentlemen were killed; and so few saved.'*

### G1: Levy pikeman, Arran's ward

This figure broadly illustrates Patten's description. He wears an iron skull cap beneath his bonnet, which bears the oak-and-saw livery badge, and a neckerchief is wound several times around his neck under the jack. Unusually, he carries as sidearms not only a conventional 'bollock' dagger but also an imported German basilard with what is now called a 'Holbein' hilt. His buckler is strapped to his left forearm in such a manner to allow him to carry his pike with both hands.

### G2: Banner-bearer, Clan Dury

He carries what was most likely the banner of George Dur Abbot of Dunfermline, described by Patten as follows: *banner of white sarsenet on which was painted a woma with her hair about her shoulders, kneeling before a crucif and on her right hand a church after that written along upo the banner in great roman letters AFFLICTAE SPONSAE, N OBLIVISCARIS! (Forget Not Your Afflicted Wife)'*

The next most important feature to note about this figur is that he is a well-born officer, thus illustrating Patten's poir that men of all classes wore very similar gear. His helmet is 'war hat', here an example from the Kelvingrove collectior with a raised central comb. The jacket is a brigandine covered with white leather and fastened with straps an buckles up the left side. It is lined with small metal plate secured by rivets of gilt latten (a copper alloy) through th material, appearing in straight lines. Its laced-on sleeves ar protected by 'splints' – interlinked iron bars, rings an elbow-pieces sewn in place; and note on the left uppe sleeve the Dury's yellow crescent badge. Beneath the brigandine his throat is protected by a mail collar c 'standard'. His fine quality sword has thumb-rings at the hil and would be balanced by a dagger on the right hip.

### G3: Rattler

Patten also describes a couple of more unusual items foun in the Scottish camp after the battle:

*'They were new boards' ends cut off being about a foot i breadth and half a yard in length; having on the insid handles made very cunningly of two cord lengths. These r Gods name were their targets against the shot of our sma artillery for they were not able to hold out a cannon...*

*'And with these were found great rattles, swelling bigge than a belly of a pottle [half-gallon] pot covered with ol parchment or double paper, small stones put in them to mak a noise and set upon a staff more than two ells long. And th was their fine device to frighten our horses, when ou horsemen should come at them. Howbeit because the rider were no babies nor their horses any colts they could neithe duddle the one nor affray the other. So that this policy was a witless as their power forceless.'*

The third figure depicts a burgh man assessing hi chances should he be asked to carry these items in comba it is little wonder that they seem to have been left at th

Today, St Mary's at Haddington (see Plate H) bears the scars of the artillery duel fought between the Scots, who had mounted cannons in the tower, and the English within the town's defences. (Author's collection)

### H1: German mercenary captain

This figure, based on a woodcut by Doring c.1550, depicts a captain of Philip Rhinegrave von Salm's mercenaries who fought at Haddington. He wears fully articulated Nuremberg half-armour except on his right arm; the left, being the 'leading' arm in combat, is protected by pauldrons, rerebraces and vambraces. The breast shows the developing trend of the 'peascod' , with the front ridge drawn out and down forming a prominent peak; by 1540 the apex was higher above the navel.

### H2: Spanish caliverman

This figure is taken from Vermeyen's 'Conquest of Tunis' dated 1535. The troops chosen for the assault were ordered to wear their shirts over their outer clothing to ensure easy recognition. He wears his equipment over the shirt; typically, he would wind a spare length of slowmatch around his forearm. The primary weapon is an early petronel or caliver with its distinctive curved butt.

### H3: Italian mercenary

The Italian soldier is based on woodcuts of 1530 by David De Necker; his plumed hat and puffed and slashed doublet and breeches are very similar to contemporary German Landsknecht fashions. This man has reversed his 'cassack', wearing it inside out to show the white linen lining for the night assault (the cassack slipped over the head like a tabard, and the front section is tucked under the waist belt). His harquebus is of German origin; note that he wears a round brass powder flask slung around his neck.

### H4: Highland archer

Jean de Beaugué, serving as an officer in the French army at Haddington, described the Highland contingent as they entered the trenches: *They [Highland chieftains] were followed by several highlanders; and these last go almost naked – they have stained [painted] shirts and sort of woollen covering, variously coloured, and are armed like the rest with large bows, broadswords and targets'.* There is some debate as to the type of bows carried by Highlanders. Contemporary illustrations by Dürer and Holinshead depict the 'wild Scots' carrying recurved bows; but Beaugué specifically describes them as 'large', inferring the use of the 'war' bow of their English counterparts. The 'broadswords' mentioned by Beague had blades retaining the same width down to the point in the Irish manner, with simple rounded pommels, leather-bound handgrips, and straight, squared-off quillons.

camp. Again, he wears a Hamilton badge on his bonnet. His sleeveless, thigh-length jack of plates is covered in white fustian rather than leather, with white linen lining; it is the stitching to hold the plates in place that gives the material a quilted effect. This example is fastened down the front by means of six hooks-and-eyes, and displays the usual saltire. His arms are protected against cuts by thin chains of latten stitched along the length of his doublet sleeves. Typical personal items might be the rosary at his belt, a canvas haversack, and some kind of proofed leather waterbottle.

## H: SIEGE OF HADDINGTON, 1548–49

A multi-national Scottish army laid much of East Lothian to waste in an attempt to destroy the English 'Pale' set up in the town; the Scots were supported by French, German, Dutch, Spanish and Italian mercenaries. The English were finally forced to abandon the town as the garrison, starving and ravaged by plague, could not be resupplied effectively. St Mary's parish church, shown in the background, lay just outside the fortress, and was – perhaps foolishly – left standing by the English before the siege began. The building became a focal point of the fighting in the following months; the French used it as a forward gun position, and the English spent valuable shot trying to displace them. The French launched a particularly determined night attack from the church on 10 October 1548 – a 'camisado', so-called from the practice of wearing white shirts for visibility and friend-and-foe identification in the dark. The raiders breached the outer base court of the fortress before being repulsed with heavy losses, suffered at the muzzle of a double-shotted cannon reputedly fired by a Frenchman fighting for the English.

# INDEX